~~MONUMENT~~

Other books by Bonny Cassidy

Certain Fathoms
Final Theory
Chatelaine

BONNY CASSIDY

~~MONUMENT~~

First published 2024
from the Writing and Society Research Centre
at Western Sydney University
by the Giramondo Publishing Company
PO Box 752
Artarmon NSW 1570 Australia
www.giramondopublishing.com

© Bonny Cassidy 2024

Cover image: Benjamin Duterrau (1767–1851). *The Conciliation* 1840 (detail), oil. Purchased with assistance from the Friends of the Tasmanian Museum and Art Gallery and the Murray Fund, 1945. Collection: Tasmanian Museum and Art Gallery. AG79.

Designed by Jenny Grigg
Typeset by Andrew Davies
in Tiempos Regular 9/15pt

Printed and bound by SOS Print+Media
Distributed in Australia by NewSouth Books

A catalogue record for this
book is available from the
National Library of Australia.

ISBN 978-1-922725-89-9

All rights reserved.
No part of this publication may be
reproduced, stored in a retrieval
system or transmitted in any form or
by any means electronic, mechanical,
photocopying or otherwise without the
prior permission of the publisher.

9 8 7 6 5 4 3 2 1

The Giramondo Publishing Company acknowledges the support of Western Sydney University in the implementation of its book publishing program.

This project has been assisted by the Commonwealth Government through the Australia Council, its arts funding and advisory body.

First Nations readers are advised that this book contains the names of people who have passed away. It includes references to frontier violence, racist language and colonial trauma.

'...the history of this country has been so uneventful.'

Gold everlastings
and shadow.

I'd a class in half an hour. At Victoria Street I hopped off my bike and walked it the last hundred metres to the campus. I was seeing as I did in the city, into some noisy, close horizon.

I talked a lot about history
but imagined I didn't have one

I talked a lot about Whiteness
hoping to come home to

White another smokescreen
another spell to cast emptiness

Paused at the traffic lights, my eyes habitually sought the gate of Old Melbourne Gaol. But in that usual line of sight, something new stood out.

The pedestrian alarm bleeped me onwards. Where I normally pushed straight through to the laneway that led into the campus – my path was interrupted.

I edged the bike closer and circled.

Dug into the footpath was a loosely fenced garden. Inside it, paving. And a high frame made of steel, like a kids' swingset. A row of primary-coloured boxes resembling New York newspaper vendors.

It's a new playground, I thought. Facing the basalt roar of the gaol's entrance, it was a strange site: three lanes of city traffic passed one side; on the other, the uni campus offered more appealing corners for covert pashing and smoking.

A crushed silvereye; its silhouette of motion.

From the top of the steel frame, chains dropped to a gunmetal granite block set on the ground. Instead of being loosely attached to swinging seats, the chains were taut, hooked to the granite. On the block were inscribed two words:

TUNNERMINNERWAIT *MAULBOYHEENER*

I stepped towards the colourful vendors. The flow of traffic revved through its timed phases.

    I tried to open the bright boxes; they were fixed. Each had a window through which I could see a metal plaque. Each plaque was printed with text – fragments of stories, those names that I stumbled to say.

It took me a while to grasp why the plaques of text were fixed behind windows.

I recalled a walk I had taken back in 2010 while writing my poetry book, *Final Theory*. I had followed a trail around Lake St Clair in lutruwita, Tasmania, where signs pointed out Palawa food sources and routes. But I hadn't been able to read the words or illustrations on the metal signs because each of them had been slashed

Standing at the monument, I balanced my bike with one hand while I checked my phone for the time. My class was due to start any minute.

I tapped a search into the browser. The image loaded in my palm. I held the screen up beside the monument.

The sandy hillock and the granite block; the skyward spears and the steel chains; the bare skin and the city pavement. The friendly hand.

The monument had turned down the traffic's volume. Embedded in my path, it pulsed

The House Under the Hill

South-east Van Diemen's Land
(1820–1852)

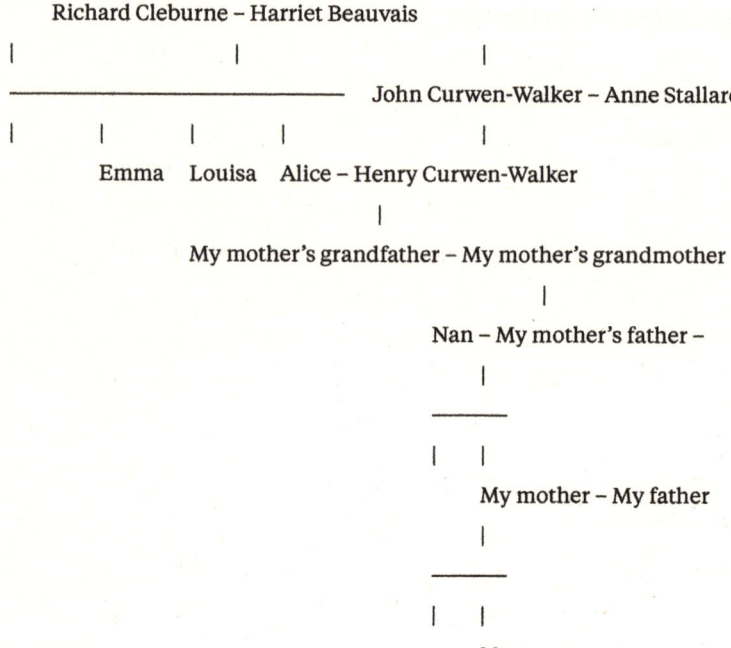

In the 1830s two young Palawa men, Tunnerminnerwait and Maulboyheener meet George Augustus Robinson, Chief Protector of Aborigines for Van Diemen's Land.

Tunnerminnerwait is a Parperloihener man of the north-west coastal nation of lutruwita, Tasmania. As a child he witnessed a massacre of his people at Cape Grim. Maulboyheener is of the Panpekanner group from the north-east tip of the island. He has never known his younger brother, who was taken as an infant from their mother by the English squatter, John Batman. Robinson is an Englishman, a builder by trade, tall with a good deal of strong flab. He keeps a journal.

His story is raked over by historians and writers. Robinson seems to be eternally fascinating and inscrutable to us whitefellas. We have hoped him to have been some sort of noble settler, and yet.

The Governor of Van Diemen's Land has given him a mission, to meet all Palawa groups and persuade them to join a settlement at Flinders Island in the Bass Strait. Robinson proposes that the Palawa be permitted a reserve on Van Diemen's Land so that they can remain closer to Country, but the Governor rejects the suggestion. The land is too valuable and the danger too risky – to everybody – he says. The Governor much prefers the idea of sending Robinson off into the forest. He never expects the Chief Protector to return, let alone walk into Hobart one day with a deputation of clan leaders.

Trudging around the island on foot, covering unfamiliar distances and negotiating meetings, Robinson is plagued by rashes during his journey through the estuaries and forests. He sneaks away from camp before dawn to wash, imagining he can't be seen. His most treasured thing is the rucksack containing his journals of names, language, customs and travels: the journals are intelligence, and his legacy.

Robinson introduces himself to as many Palawa as he can. If they'll just stick with him, Robinson reassures Tunnerminnerwait, Maulboyheener and the others he meets, they will be able to return to their homelands later. He knows this isn't what the Governor has agreed to, but Robinson is confident enough in his own powers to believe he can make it so.

And what do the Palawa believe? Their warrior ranks are shrinking, elderly and kids are getting left behind in the warfare, and the number of settlers is rapidly multiplying. How do the Palawa, daily and in diverse groups, negotiate between their will to survive and any settler's offer of trust? We know that they accept Robinson's promise to return them home, because of their outrage when he later breaks it.

As for me, I want to believe that Robinson is a true friend, not just a jumped-up chancer or a creepy preacher. Are his efforts of uncomfortable travel, intercultural friendship, language learning – things attempted by no other non-Palawa – really only made for the rewards of status and a salary? I want to believe that, knowing the apocalypse has already come to the Palawa, Robinson is building a safe place for them. And yet.

Robinson returns to the Governor with representatives from his 'friendly mission'. They walk through Hobart. Before they sail to Flinders Island, Tunnerminnerwait and Maulboyheener have their likenesses painted by the leading society portraitist, Thomas Bock. They are joined by Truganini, born on Bruny Island and wife of Wurati. They are also sketched by Benjamin Duterrau, who tells them he will put them into a painting with their Chief Protector.

The Flinders Island settlement, Wybalenna, is formed in 1834. Overseen at first by Robinson, its residents come from different homelands across Van Diemen's Land yet are made to cohabit and work together under inspection. They comply with the roster of gardening, manufacture, worship and cleaning, while trying to maintain independent hunting and camping trips away from the settlement. And in just five years Wybalenna is rife with disease and death. Remote and offshore, run to a foreign moral code, language and roster of activity, it is what we now recognise as, at best, a permanent detention centre; at worst, a concentration camp.

At the deepening of his friends' misery, Robinson chooses to move on. In what seems like a sudden attack of fatalism, cowardly embarrassment, or ambitious opportunism – or all three – he takes up as Chief Protector of Aborigines in Port Phillip, across the Bass Strait.

He tries to keep the relationships going with his closest friends from Wybalenna. In 1839, along with eleven others, Robinson asks Truganini and Wurati, plus Maulboyheener, Tunnerminnerwait and his wife Planobeena to accompany him as cultural liaisons at Port Phillip. They agree to go.

In their absence, things only worsen at Wybalenna. A series of punitive commanders is hired. The remaining Palawa resist. They are becoming increasingly aware that they will not be returning home, and that their good faith in the state's mission has been abused. They leap the chain of colonial command: Maulboyheener's elder brother Walter leads a petition to Queen Victoria to protest the community's treatment.

Meanwhile, Tunnerminnerwait accompanies Robinson in his new role on the mainland. They travel to the west of Port Phillip, into Wathaurong and Gunditjmara lands.

Once he returns to Melbourne, though, Tunnerminnerwait keeps travelling. He joins with Maulboyheener, Planobeena, Truganini and another woman, Pyterruner. They move east around Port Phillip, in the opposite direction to Robinson, along Boon Wurrung Country to Western Port and Dandenong. Stations are ransacked and people assaulted. Eventually the Palawa group is apprehended for murdering two whalers.

Before Robinson's mission, Truganini and her family were viciously attacked by sailors, sealers, soldiers and timber-getters back at their home on Bruny Island. All the southern coastal nations' relationships with whalers and sealers have been long, complicated and bloody. The mainland murders will often be interpreted as a long-awaited reprisal. Maybe the slain whalers stand in for those who got away at Bruny; or maybe the Palawa group track and assassinate their targets across hundreds of kilometres of sea and soil. Or maybe they are now using violence and theft because, in the end, it seems the only language that invaders understand. I think of Trawlwoolway artist Julie Gough's image, *Manifestation (Bruny Island)*: a dining chair pierced by a spear, both on fire. They're extinguishing one another on a rock shelf beside an estuary.

In court at Port Phillip, the Palawa travellers are not invited to testify for themselves. Robinson is the only witness in their defence. The three women are let off by the jury, but Tunnerminnerwait and

Maulboyheener are sentenced for murder. In 1842, they are hanged before a huge crowd at Victoria Street, outside what is now the Old Melbourne Gaol.

There isn't a chance for the travellers in that foreign courtroom to unfold their story, which is much bigger than murdered whalers at Western Port.

Their story isn't mine, but I am standing by it.

John Curwen-Walker is the first to turn up. He wanders the perimeter of the room, sliding past paintings that've been hauled up from storage.

Benjamin Duterrau is dead. The second wind of fame he expected from Van Diemen's Land is blowing past his cold studio, towards this tawdry auction room.

A kitten! Waifs! A horse. Peasants with baskets. Curwen-Walker shakes his head. This is the dross his friend Ben excelled at. Imagine having been given a talent to produce the stuff nobody wanted, stuff that bored even yourself. The artist's sister fidgets on a chair in the back corner.

When he and Ben first met at the Mechanics Institute, Curwen-Walker had been dreaming of a picture. Something suitable for his bank office, a legacy commission. The image had kept returning to his mind: a tableau of the different classes of Van Diemonian, showing their improvement of character over forty years since the colony began. It could even have a title to help the viewer, he'd thought, in case they missed the cues: 'The Making of History' or 'The Road to Reason', something like that. And Curwen-Walker's favourite detail, a secret gift to himself: a tiny image of his own likeness deep inside the picture – his face just visible in the bank window above Liverpool Street.

With his vision, Curwen-Walker had gone to Ben's place. He'd stood in the studio and pretended to sip the awful chicory coffee. With his free hand, Curwen-Walker had blocked out his imagined composition while Ben squinted. Curwen-Walker had outlined a slope, the Hobart foothills. Arranged up the incline would be the various characters at their business, he went on: a pair of grizzled old natives playing in the shallows at the bottom, a convict gang bent at work on the city foundations, a merchant directing loads into his warehouse above the docks, then three or four young daughters of gentry, promenad –

Ben had held up his palm. He'd stopped squinting. He could hear his sister gently moving furniture upstairs, which meant she was listening through the floorboards. 'Back to the natives a moment,' the artist had said.

Curwen-Walker had nodded eagerly, his vision becoming reality. 'Yes, perhaps an old couple of men, begging or even simply watching the progress. Symbolically they represent –'

'Forget the city,' Ben had stated bluntly. 'See? Let's have our difficult hero and his suffering friends. Yes!' He'd raised an index finger. '*Robinson and the Aborigines*. There's your picture,' and nodded, as though it were decided. The floorboards upstairs had gone silent.

Politely, with much back-patting and chin-stroking, Curwen-Walker had declined Ben Duterrau's counterproposal. He'd gone on his way, forgotten his dream picture. The two remained friends, and Ben did some portraits of the Curwen-Walker children. But as the kids started to enter polite society, Curwen-Walker wondered if he had done the right thing in laughing off Ben's history painting.

The artist wanted to leave behind an epic – his national picture. Curwen-Walker remembers him railing at the lectern, and then railing in the newspaper, and finally just railing at his friends to band together and fund a painting that would represent the pivotal moment of Van Diemen's Land. The moment that George

Augustus Robinson convinced the natives to give up the fight and go with him to the island.

Robinson himself loved the idea of the painting. Encouraged, Ben went to sketch the Palawa at Robinson's house, mocking up gestures and stances to show various attitudes in what Robinson called the Palawa's 'conciliation'. But nobody fronted up to pay Benjamin Duterrau a commission for the work.

While he carried on churning out schlocky portraits and scenes, Ben privately continued to work on his national picture. First, he made a large version, big enough for a wealthy parlour or lobby, a test of composition and colour. Then he completed the full-scale painting, taller than a man and wide as a drawing room.

In the auction room, Curwen-Walker stands before the two versions. He checks the list of works in his hand – no starting prices.

It isn't the first time he's seen Ben's final arrangement of the composition. After a polite pause following his failed proposal, the artist started showing Curwen-Walker his studies for it, some of which are also hanging here on the auction room's walls. The intimacy of their wonky brush marks makes Curwen-Walker smile. Despite all of Ben's preparatory work, you'd never catch Bock doing a hand like this one, or Glover doing a shrub like that.

Curwen-Walker casts a glance behind him. A few curious onlookers sit themselves down in the auction room as though it's a public park. They're unwrapping some cold lunch from a bag. Beneath a painting of a tot in rags, a smartly dressed little girl apes the pose for her mother to admire.

Has it become history yet?

Curwen-Walker fiddles with a broken bit of stick in his pocket. It fell into his hair on his way down the hill. He pierces the tip of his forefinger with it as the auctioneer begins calling for bids. The romantic scenes are being given away for a pound each. Nothing is going beyond a first bidder. In a trance of humility, Ben's sister looks into the floor.

Curwen-Walker returns his gaze to the two largest pictures in the room – the double crowd of eyes looking at one another, at Robinson, at him.

In 1851, Robinson quits the colonies altogether and sails back to England. The painter Benjamin Duterrau dies in Hobart and his storeroom of unsold paintings is auctioned, including the two versions of his unwanted 'National Picture'.

My great-great-great grandfather, John Curwen-Walker offers the highest recorded bid at the auction. It buys him the slightly smaller version, which will become known as *The Conciliation*. The larger version will never be found.

Curwen-Walker doesn't publicly show the image of Chief Protector George Augustus Robinson 'conciliating' with Tunnerminnerwait, Maulboyheener, Truganini, Wurati and other Palawa. For about ten years, *The Conciliation* hangs privately at his house on the Derwent River.

That's where it is seen by Curwen-Walker's mate, Richard Cleburne, who lives on the opposite bank of the river at Risdon Cove. Their families have become so friendly that the youngsters wave bed linen at one another across the water.

Richard Cleburne will also become my great-great-great grandfather. He doesn't start his life in Van Diemen's Land at Risdon Cove, however.

Anglo-Irish from Cork, young Cleburne busies himself in Hobart during the 1820s. He's getting married and setting up tallow, spirits and hardware businesses, buying bits of land and selling them again. He closely follows local news as the Governor of Van Diemen's Land prepares to institute three years of martial law.

The Palawa resistance to invasion is getting increasingly violent. Two groups of domestic servants are killed at Pitt Water during 1829, on the estuary east of Risdon Cove. For the first time the local Moomairremener band are hungry enough to make raids during winter. They need food to replace their lost kangaroo grounds, and they need to drive settlers away from locking up any more of their land, from killing their loved ones. In 1830, there are 124 attacks on settlers in other parts of Oyster Bay lands back from the cove.

While Richard Cleburne keeps his family safe in a Hobart townhouse, Tongerlongeter leads the 'war-hardened remnant' of the Oyster Bay nation in guerilla attacks on settlers up and down the Derwent River.

When martial law fails against this force, the Governor conceives of the Black Line campaign. Troopers and volunteers are deployed to beat the bush around Richmond and Pitt Water, and capture or kill the warriors.

Despite the lives lost on both sides, the Black Line fails, too. Knowing their Country better than anyone, small groups of Palawa with strategists like Tongerlongeter have been able to manoeuvre around the cordons.

The Governor turns to his last resort; a change of tactic. He appoints Chief Protector George Augustus Robinson to begin a diplomatic mission.

Richard Cleburne thinks about moving out of Hobart. Cleburne thinks about a family home upriver. Cleburne thinks about the quiet acres of Risdon Cove.

A far-travelling echo

reaches me from the house under the hill at Risdon Cove.

As soon as I try to recall it, though, the story refracts and squirms. It goes

she pours coals
onto the black feet and watches
the skin appear.

No –

She appears before a pair of black feet,
they turn toward her.

A pair of blackened feet runs
away. Or –

A pair of feet appears behind
and she casts the coals.

She doesn't look back
as she runs.

White coals left to blacken in the hearth.

This is the home of my great-great-great grandfather, Richard Cleburne.

I see him gliding over the Derwent on a punt. Leaving Hobart behind, he is approaching his new house with its wife and children inside.

I can picture the arable slopes around the house, free settlers growing fruit, wheat, grazing sheep.

I can see Derwent River in the foreground and the hills of hump-backed Mount Direction behind.

I see the inlet of Risdon Cove. Some of the stone huts from the first 1803 colony are lived in but looking shabby. Most of its original members fled in 1804, across to Hobart to establish the southern colony afresh.

I can see a poxy maid holding a pot and a nasty savage creeping up behind her.

The scene is forever set on pause. Like the cell of a cartoon; one-dimensional, black and white.

Legacy

Narrm, Melbourne
(2018–2022)

A monument may possess 'contiguous magic'
be amulet-like, a wish

a well that catches the heart
or anything thrown in.

It's been a few years since my first encounter with the monument. It has become a part of my map. I follow the thin lines backwards. I believe they begin in the past.

My two great-great-great-grandfathers are long gone from living memory, but traces of them have always been nearby. In marrying my mother's father (yet another John Curwen-Walker, who died before I was born), Nan lived with heirlooms and images and stories of both men and their families. My mother can also recount these tales and interiors. And since I grew up with both women, I absorbed the distant presence of Van Diemen's Land.

Brook Andrew and Trent Walter's monument *Standing by Tunnerminnerwait and Maulboyheener* was constructed in 2016. It shouldn't have surprised me as it did on my way to work that day. A couple of years before it appeared in my path, I went to a rally led by a Plangermairreenner (Ben Lomond nation) man, the writer and activist Jim Everett-puralia meenamatta, to support lobbying the City of Melbourne for the monument's construction. But I never looked up an illustration of the design, and after the rally I forgot. If I'm honest, part of me suspected that it would never be approved by the council.

I watch how, fed by exhaust and hard bitumen, the monument's native garden thrives taller and thicker.

And how, one by one, the city's monuments to colonial heroes are dissolving. Burke and Wills were removed during subway construction, and John Batman's lean visage has been put into storage. Their disappearance seems barely noticed.

I didn't grow up here. My first thirty years, my childhood with my parents and Nan, was in the legacy of another colony.

It was a middle class, suburban childhood off the edge of Camay, Botany Bay.

Cronulla was two places in one. There were the gentle, fecund foreshore of bays and reef platforms, and the raging testosterone of the Sharks stadium. In our backyards, mower-friendly buffalo grass covered dunes of sand. At night, over the booming swell, American sitcoms and blooper shows illuminated our lounge rooms.

These layers never really met one another in a way that made sense. I couldn't find any story that explained who lived there side by side, and why. Even asking the question was out of place.

The suburb has never been as White as the 2005 rioters made it out to be. Maybe not quite Fiona Foley's *Nulla 4 Eva* – but my first little mates, the ones who shared Cronulla with me, were a Gamilaroi family and second-generation Greek, Maori, Samoan, Filipino, Sri Lankan-Australian kids. There were some nice Anglo families, too, and some mean ones. I wish our attention had been drawn to the locality that brought us together.

The coast where my father surfed every day was and is embedded with antiquity. To my younger self these corners of Cronulla were mysterious and enchanting. Sandstone caves around Bass and Flinders Point, petroglyphs in the Royal National Park, and middens along Gunnamatta Bay and Bundeena, all seemingly abandoned.

They were enigmatic to me, just like the museums I loved. I read and listened with intense hunger about dinosaurs, megafauna, evolution, ornithology, archaeology, cryptozoology. Mine was a desire for the hardly believable; for a Narnia-like realm that sat just outside this one. I had no sense – I wasn't told – that the coastal culture I admired was part of Dharawal history, and that it was living.

The Redfern Speech was a sound replaying on the TV at the corner shop; Mabo was a word on the nightly news. The books of Yolngu art my mother showed me, and later the desert places our family would travel, were sublime to me but nothing to do with home. In our little paradise, the loudest voices and the visible signs of pride promoted our local connection to the founding story.

Captain Cook's face was on murals and all the council signage; his landing memorial stood on the horizon at Kurnell, and monuments to Bass and Flinders appeared around the Port Hacking River. The Bicentenary of 1788 floated on Sydney's foreshores like grease. Even if I'd known there were protests going on nearby at La Perouse, I'd have had no context to grasp their meaning.

I wasn't too young to learn about the legacy of Gweagal and Eora civilisation. To love it as a gift. To feel sick about something because I could imagine it happening to me. To feel injustice. I read Anne Frank's journal when I was about eleven. And it was a quiet afternoon when our Year 6 teacher cleared the desks and the blackboard and sat the class down in a circle on the lino tiles.

In kindergarten, terrified of interrupting, I'd peed on those tiles rather than asking to leave the room. They had been conveniently lifted away by the teacher and cleaned. Before they'd been pressed back down, I'd looked at the brown MDF: the floor beneath the floor.

That afternoon, the teacher told us as much as she could and then sent us home. As usual, my mother collected me at the playground gate. My primary schooling never referred to the Holocaust again, and before we'd had a chance to raise a hand my classmates and I were shuffled along to high school.

Today I decide to take a longer route to the university, cycling via the edge of the industrial Port of Melbourne and across the traces of Birrarung estuaries now drained and diverted.

I swish up into the CBD behind Southern Cross Station and pass a Victorian era hotel opposite the tracks, emblazoned with the name *BATMAN'S HILL*. John Batman lived there, with his chimney and bad dreams, until 1839. Later, the railway track would cut one side and the top off the hill.

I ride past the cutting, office towers squatting upon it. Adjacent the phantom hill, the colossal clay-white figure of Bruce Armstrong's *Bunjil* rests on a plinth, watching behind and ahead.

Slowing through the thick of the city grid, I see scrubbed young men in slouch hats selling Legacy badges. I whizz by silver-haired veterans and their grandchildren in miniature suits. They are moving towards Birrarung Wilam and over the river, towards the war memorial. I head in the opposite direction.

My office overlooks east Narrm, Melbourne. Bike locked and backpack dropped, I can see the yellow battlements of Trades Hall, union flags snapping. There's a helicopter buzzing high above, like a wasp trapped under the sky. And down below my window, the native rosemary is blooming around the monument, *Standing by Tunnerminnerwait and Maulboyheener.*

It's well after lunchtime when I notice a text from my mother, warning me that I'm going to get a call from my father. This is a very unusual message.

They've been married forty years, never even moved house since I was born. If she texts me about him he's usually copied in on the joke. This one sends a cold plunge into my guts.

When my father phones me, his voice is familiar, but as I listen to it trying to find words that it's never had to say before, my feet go wandering out of the office, downstairs and outside.

He tells me that he's the father of two other daughters, from two different affairs. They were born decades apart: one when my brother was an infant; and another about the time I moved out of home in my early twenties. Yes, he says, he sees them. He always has. And they have always known about us.

My feet have taken me to a courtyard across the lane from my office. It's walled in basalt bluestone that runs the edge of the Old Melbourne Gaol. A fig tree towers on top of the wall, its roots like tentacles holding the face of the storm-coloured stone. It feels right to go into a corner. I'm numb and mute, and as he stumbles on I sit beneath a cherry tree in the shade.

His families have existed in parallel dimensions since before I was born. He has moved between them, as though across a corridor – closing a door on one room and opening the door into another – until today. Within moments my closeknit family – my mother, brother, uncles and aunts, cousins – are all standing amongst fragments that were supposed to stay disconnected.

I'm leaning against the bluestone wall, holding the phone to my ear. Listening to my father's voice resisting a new story about how things are. I am learning.

His disclosure is not voluntary. He had begun to have difficulty keeping all the lies together. My mother had found other people's belongings in the home, which in isolation didn't tell a story – and pushed him to explain. Now, his explanation comes to me as a stammer, a half-languaged thing.

For him, it is a story about the past.
But as Paul Riceour writes in *Memory, History, Forgetting* 'one does not remember alone'.
Despite himself, my father brings me into his remembering.

I am watching myself from above, a figure weaving through a forest. And I am in the undergrowth.

Rage, disgust. Heartbreak, disbelief. Grief, letting go. They will visit me in succession, there are seasons and years. Some bits of me will sprout; others toughen or decay.

After a year or so of tidal anger, I feel a flood of compassion for my father.

Compassion is a strange emotion, or an idea of the heart. It is neither forgiveness nor care. Once it's released into the body it cannot be revoked.

At that moment I know I've accepted what was shocking. Whatever it makes me feel, I must draw it into my world, however I can. It is a gradual process, but denial is so much more painful. 'To deny what was…you don't even need to suppress many of the facts; you only need to remove the link that connects them and constitutes them as a story,' says Jacques Rancière.

When I think about it that way, there is no choice. My world has gotten bigger. It's too soon to forget.

I sit in the bluestone courtyard on the phone, until my father's story is done. Then I speak: I tell my father to get some counselling, and I hang up.

The top of my head feels open, my legs and feet seem heavy. It is gone, my little world – the way I remember my family, my sense of knowing him.

I sit for a while longer. The muscly roots of the fig tree appear to grow from the masonry, anchoring the Old Gaol wall to the ground beneath the concrete.

Behind me
on the other side of this wall, is the monument

built to remind us of denial
the big and the little kinds
that tear us apart

as well as what we remember together
collect and corroborate

what we don't want to know.

My aunt gives me a badge that says
I AM A MONUMENT
but I can't bring myself to

carry around this word.

Look for somewhere
to place a few pebbles;
any day is the right one.

The monument told me to stand up and pay attention to where I was walking. It told me that I was standing by the past, always.

Like how history between people and places *really* happens – a million frontiers.

I crouch near the ground
leaves and granules spread about
reminding me that every place I know is already graven.

Remembering is not about repetition. It is about re-reading history that is not yet ready to be forgotten, 'delving beneath what the words say and dredging up what they say without thinking, what they say as monuments as opposed to what they say intentionally'.

I arrive again. The history once obscured by elevated figures still lies in shadow

and they move amongst us and we barely notice.

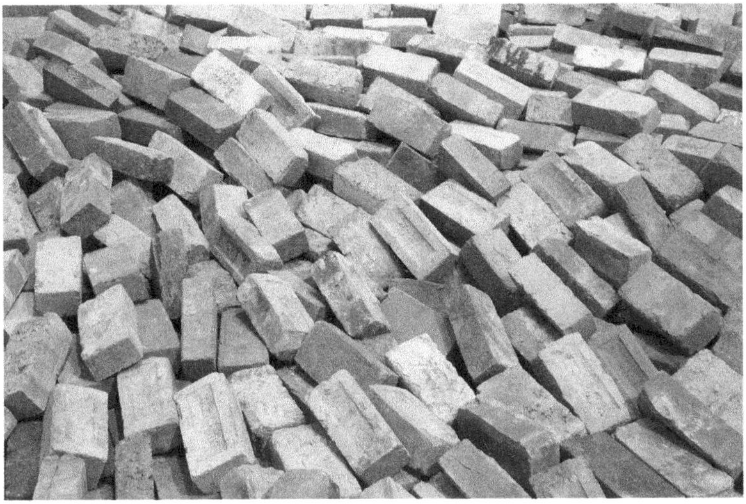

Blackwood

Western District, Victoria
(1840–1920)

Johann Gottlieb Anders – Pauline Heinicke
　　　|
　――――――
|　　　|
　　　Herman Anders – Eliza Layfield – – –
　　　|
　　　Emily Anders – Jabez Squire – – –
　　　　　|
　　　　　――――――― – – – –
　　　　　|　　　|
　　　　　Nan –
　　　　　|

A first generation arrives many times over

their firstness itself is not really a story:
the story is what they entered

into

Wybalenna is miles behind him, it is lodged in his brain like a stone.

When Chief Protector Robinson turns up at Port Phillip, it's considered a colony within New South Wales – the southern limit of Sydney. Port Phillip means whaling along the wild southern coast, centred on Portland to the western end; and grazing through the lush, gold grasslands than run up from the edge to the base of the highlands. Whaling means itinerant workers, mixed-race communities, and peak enterprise. Sail in sail out. Grazing means convict and ex-convict workers, feudal overseers, and unchecked land use.

Both industries rely on First Nations' labour and knowledge of sea and land. Both needed the un-granted, extractive use of their hunting, farming and harvesting grounds. The grounds that encompassed seasonal settlements of stone huts below the old volcano Budj Bim, the thatched sheds and piles of eels beside Lake Bolac, creation and ceremony sites in the caves and gorges of Gariwerd.

Tunnerminnerwait chooses to accompany Robinson. One purpose of their trip west is to investigate the 'Convincing Ground' at Portland, where a massacre of Kilcarer gundidj by whalers has been reported. Robinson hopes that Tunnerminnerwait will act as a diplomatic aide, as he did during the mission in Van Diemen's Land. But the Parperloihener man isn't always welcome or comfortable in the company of unknown languages and lands. I notice that he often diplomatically exits Robinson's encounters and, thereby, the journal. What history does Tunnerminnerwait want to make?

Robinson's journal entries from the Western District are suspicious but civil, curious yet hardened. From his perspective, every meeting with a settler glimmers with the possibility of violence. Every crossroad or passerby presents Robinson with equal chances of hospitality and aggression. 'All was not right.'

Whether or not he brings justice, Robinson wants to write it. He is making a monument, perhaps not the kind he intends. What I see in his journal pages isn't a Great Ethnographic Document, but a rough capture of voices and motivations that never quite meet one another. Sometimes purposefully, sometimes unwittingly, Robinson teaches us to read against the grain of founding stories – the story of John Batman the treaty-maker, for instance, or of Robinson the Conciliator himself. What and who needed a Protector, his journals seem to be suggesting, and from what and whom?

Back in Van Diemen's Land, he had seen the Palawa peoples' fear and resistance to his mission. He understood that they had been defending their Countries. And yet, 'he was also trying to convince himself that they had to be removed from their homeland to prevent their extermination'. Here in Port Phillip he is conciliating with himself.

The historian Inga Clendinnen concludes that Robinson, like my father, suffers cognitive dissonance: 'an uncomfortable condition in which a mind veers and twists as it strives to navigate between essential but mutually incompatible beliefs'. It is the only way she can explain Robinson's 'lurches, and swerves' of empathy.

In 1853, that spot claimed as Batman's Hill in Port Phillip is stolen for a second time – by the newly invented Victorian Government.

It's thirteen years since Robinson travelled into foreign lands with Tunnerminnerwait. Eleven years, since Tunnerminnerwait and Maulboyheener were hanged in the street. Robinson has returned to England.

The First Nations population of Victoria is estimated at 2500.
The population of settlers has increased by 50,000 in one year.
They have six million sheep, cattle and horses.
A thousand packs of guns and seven million bricks arrive.
Grains and preserved fish
grindstones, instruments and leather. Thousands of plants and seeds come from the UK and US, tonnes of salt.
Wooden houses from Britain and its colonies.

In return, Victoria exports wool and gold far beyond the quantity of any other local product.

So says the annual ledger. Before reserves are established by the state protectorate in the 1860s, the Victorian census doesn't count First Nations people without a fixed address, so it doesn't count those who are working itinerantly or living at the fringes of stations. That describes many people in the early 1850s – some of them are instead recorded as massacre headcounts in station managers' journals, and as public corroboree performers in newspapers. Others escape the colonial pen.

It doesn't pay for the state of Victoria to count too well. Blurring of the colony's boundaries is essential to its expansion. Squatters' estates are too vast for them to know closely, yet the loss of a few sheep or cattle to hunters is punishable by murder. The 'severance' of Victoria as a state 'could only be properly effected if the land was severed not only from one's own but from everyone else's lives.'

The first generation of my family to arrive in Victoria is not the one to witness or participate in the massacres and reprisals, the destruction of the villages. But the places my family occupy are witness and are marked with scars for those who care to look. The surviving custodians of those places are seen and known by settlers but denied by and removed from the sight of the state. My forebears walk in the ruins that invasion has created for them.

I begin after their memories. And yet, I know little of them except imported place names such as *Hexham*. Somehow, their memories are never properly told in the first place. Somehow, over half a century after the anthropologist W.E.H. Stanner described a national 'cult of forgetfulness', I find myself and my own family are exemplary members.

'Tell me what it means to be a white person...beyond a notion of racial superiority', asks the Gunditjmara artist and writer, Paola Balla. It doesn't mean wool or gold, or trains loaded with wheat or passengers, or freight ships loaded with my Nikes and Volkswagens.

What I have, what I mean, is unknowing. Too much forgetting has been done for me. Perhaps that's all it means to be a White person.

There was to be no *Puberty Blues* for me. While we carried on living in Cronulla, my parents agreed that my getting of wisdom was to take place elsewhere.

At the age of twelve my lifeworld was relocated to the mossy cuts and urine-puddled lanes of eastern Sydney. Five days a week, I'd ride a train for an hour from Cronulla to Kings Cross. Then emerge from the underground, some sort of lost Charles Blackman schoolgirl, to the sleepless *COCA-COLA* sign and the streetwalkers of Darlinghurst.

For my first high school assignment, my English teacher had provided the questions.

I turned on the dictaphone, setting into motion the reels of the cassette that I was to hand in the next day.

I chose Nan because she was there.

She had been there in our house since I was born. My earliest memory was of lying on my back in a navy blue, sprung perambulator with huge white wheels, as Nan pushed it around the neighbourhood.

When I could walk, we would pause to rest on a garden wall or beside the cenotaph. She'd unwrap the Jatz and liverwurst she'd brought from home.

When I started school she made me crumbed lambs' brains on weekends. She tended the garden and visited her GP for conversation.

And when she was too frail to do those things, she ordered in boxes of Beefeater and watched the tennis. She listened to Alan Jones most days. As her hearing grew worse, his voice grew louder.

I dutifully asked the provided questions, and Nan dutifully answered. She seemed to enjoy herself.

After she died, I discovered most of her answers to my assignment were framed by gentle lies.

Nan's family arrives in the Western District, where Robinson and Tunnerminnerwait walked, at the turn of the twentieth century.

What didn't she tell me? As if I could find the answer inscribed there, I drive west across Victoria.

A golf course tumbles to the rim of an enormous lake. I imagine all the little white balls, playfully hitting the surface before fading down. I close Google Maps to concentrate on the road as it slows through the town of Camperdown, borderland of the Western District. I see that the app calls the town 'historically significant'. Wouldn't want to be caught anywhere uneventful.

The kids on Manifold Street are about ten. Focused intently on their teacher, they shoot hands upwards, point at things in the street, and scribble factoids onto their worksheets. They get it: these stories imply them, explain them. Are awaiting them.

They tour a row of monuments that stand between bakeries and hairdressers. I watch the kids stand in the shadow of the Boer War, the Great War, the Celtic Cross, and the town's founding father, J.C. Manifold himself.

I keep driving out of the town, following signs to the cemetery.

A couple of juvenile magpies carefully spy the stones for snakes. The largest grave could just as easily be one of those in the centre of Camperdown: a towering obelisk hewn of blocks, a pyramid perched on top, and wrought iron fencing around its raised base. Unlike the main street's monuments, this one shows boomerangs flying upwards.

I imagine them raining down on the district ten, twenty, thirty,
forty years after Robinson visited
>   *the legitimate property of the Aborigines, who were disinherited.*

In the 1870s Wombeetch Puyuun and the Djargurd Wurrung at
Camperdown inform the Scottish farmer and linguist James
Dawson about their winter homes
>   *old residences*

built near the earthen mounds of ovens. Dawson and his daughter
Isabella learn that
>   *formed with a frame of stout limbs*
>   *the family mansion was abandoned and shut up for a season*

and roofed with stone shingles. The days are lengthening. Most
of their relations pressured to move to Framlingham reserve,
Wombeetch Puyuun and the old people who stay at Camperdown
teach James and Isabella the Djargurd Wurrung and neighbouring
dialects. In the 1880s Dawsons writes it down
>   *and I am more inclined to pin my faith to their tale*
>   *then to the coat-tail of white men tinged with druidical notions.*

Tinged with a different language of violence than before. Now it
is stealthy: increasingly strict missions and the first systematic
snatching of children. Here in the Western District of Victoria
the language of First Nations resistance has shifted from guerilla
attack, to letters from mothers to the protectorate and petitions
by activists to the state government. By sharing knowledge with
settlers like the Dawsons who'll listen, Wombeetch Puyuun acts
strategically before he dies in 1883.

The new residences of Camperdown decline to donate funds for the memorial's granite, citing the cost of
wallpaper.

Here is Dawson's mansion for Wombeetch Puyuun – half-gravestone, half-monument, half-private, half-public. I gather polyester petals and a falcon's striped tail feather from the grass, piling them up at the foot of the obelisk.

When she referred to the places of her childhood, Nan didn't tell me this story. James Dawson dies in 1900, about the time her mother and grandparents prepare to arrive at their next hotel and farm in the Western District.

As I head west from Camperdown and towards the farm, I can see the reflective oval of the lake, Gnotuk, through my greasy rear window. It hangs serenely inside a volcanic crater.

Perhaps nobody in her family knows the story of Wombeetch Puyuun and Dawson. Perhaps I am barking up the wrong tree. In the early 1900s Nan's family is leaving the Wimmera Mallee behind and moving to a place called Hexham, where they will find three mounds that 'had been extensively used, the soil at each site black and sterile' from many meals.

What do they know?

Nan knows something about the Chief Protector, George Augustus Robinson. Her husband – my mother's father – descends from Richard Cleburne and John Curwen-Walker. He is heir to the picture of Robinson and the Palawa, Benjamin Duterrau's *The Conciliation*. Whether or not Nan ever sees the painting, she hears all about its life at the Cleburne home in Risdon Cove.

But that's not what she knows. A century before my mother's father will inherit the picture, Robinson stands on the riverbank of Nan's own childhood.

From the hillside at Hexham I'm looking into the intersection of Girai Wurrung, Djab Wurrung and Wathaurong estates. While Nan dawdled nearby, my great-great-grandfather, Herman Anders works land that is fed by their confluence.

Herman's granddaughter, Nan is the last of my lineage to eat this soil. She only marries into the Van Diemen's Land story, after all.

I doubt Nan knows that, outside her grandfather Herman's inn at Hexham, a Girai Wurrung eel trap crossed the Hopkins River. Seventy years earlier, Robinson had drawn it in his journal.

They make a childish weave, the lines that I draw from this hillside – between the trap, the inn, the river, the journal, the picture. They pull out in all directions; I struggle to draw them tight.

'We can either learn from history or fall in love with the bedtime story of its deception and repeat it endlessly,' writes Bruce

Pascoe about the Western District. 'Most of your parents and grandparents never had the courage or the tools but you have access to both.'

To unlearn deception. My lines are tracing over the histories that are already here; learning them, sharpening them, missing them, stories that connect with and cross one another.

My great-great-grandfather Herman Anders knows before
he arrives in Hexham that 'the last corroboree was staged in
1862, about two miles outside, for the amusement of the white
conquerors'. There are a lot of lasts around here, after all: the type
he finds on obelisks and studio portraits, they pass unseen
>	('let others tell the tale I cannot').

/

By the time he calls it home, really there's 'no evidence' of earlier
settlement to the passing gaze. Even the squatter's run at Hexham
Park has been gridded up for selectors like him. What he thinks
of as home, as himself, becomes 'homogenised' and the soil takes
him in like it always does. The famous, molten loam is fed by
soaks and southern storms; working in this lushness there are no
gaps and no time for gaps. In this industry he becomes a bronze
monument by a highway.

/

'Where gaps exist within historical narratives, monuments act as
filler,' and so 'the monument has been the commonest answer to
the absence of continuity' in the colonised environment.

Gaps are rising from where the water table rushes up, climbing
the stones, ponds floating within mounds of basalt and bulls
standing knee-deep in red mud. Rising to the high emu plains,
big sky weighing down on cypress windbreaks. He follows the
Hopkins River down, the skin of lakes flashing clouds.

Behind the greasy sheep under his crowds
of wheat, beside a graveyard the drained swamp.

A gazette of Hexham, disintegrated into neat selections, is
dominated by the Hopkins as it inscribes itself through the land.
The river makes even the alphabet turn sideways, bobbing down
the page.

/

There are ways to read inwards, and beneath what he's told.

When he arrives, in fact, and looks closer he meets signs of a
long-cultivated land: 'the pastures consist of native grasses, and
the character of the soil and climate keep the grass growing right
through the season'. Kangaroo apple, yellow box and tea-tree
wild by the roadside and around the graveyard, thickly tangled.
Discarded bark and sapling roofs are to be cleared out from the
blackwood stands, and basalt bricks to be dragged from ovens
into borderlines. And before long, he learns that 'the former
camps of the natives are now mostly grassed over…at Hexham
Park, on the Hopkins River'. Every day he passes the sunken
stretch as he enters the village, open flats leading up to the river
banks. Ducks scramble from the shady water as he approaches.

He calls the spot *Weetya* for that Djab Wurrung blackwood

and no one asks how he acquires this word for a place of trees that
covers him in planets of light as he makes the boundaries of his
living.

When he travels out his gate, he takes the old eel highway through Girrae Wurrung land, from Hexham to Lake Bolac. Kestrels and herons work over the tributaries of the river, following the fish runs. Salt Creek remains lush, there's a small storage pool on its floodbank. He may hear of the lava flows in Gunditjmara Country, their villages of stone in bracken to the west. A smoking gum. Inside the ashes of its gut, its fat, steady fire, and the rain in its muscles like sleep. An old-timer may tell him that where his pub stands near the ford at Hexham, is where George Augustus Robinson noted a weir of sticks erected to snare the shortfin eel as the waters rose.

He has witnessed evidence of what one surveyor calls 'a dateless monument of incredible labour'. But he forgets it gradually, because there's 'no recognition of the process of displacement that was occurring' for generations before he got there.

Those gaps between what's known and denied, seen and forgotten, close up. He says nothing to his grandchildren; and so it's as though he has always been here. Bulrushes fill the clearing.

From the crushed oven mounds, his sons collect flakes and glass, and keep them precious on a windowsill. They draw a pair of scarred trees, still there, further up the river where it turns into the town. Historian Maggie Mackellar writes that 'first-generation Australians were blind to the transnational encounters that were happening all the time' in the lands they'd invaded. Their progeny are bestowed with an immediate inheritance. 'In spring on open country they watched for the first blue orchids and in sheltered places sought greenhoods. They climbed hollow trees to find parrots' nests...they could fish the creeks for yabbies and on summer evenings sit, bare toes in the water, listening to the croak of frogs and the shrilling of crickets. They could hunt wallabies, possums and bears, and make rugs from their skins.' Everything else is the past.

/

His forgetting is a basalt pool where he might drop.

Lying down. In a place where he remade himself.

Hexham means he's neither the district record for 2000 sacks of heroic wheat, nor a patriarch. He's a guest, gathering leeches as he dwells in the Country that feeds him.

Ross Gibson insists that 'remembering is something good we can do in response to the bad in our lands'. Memory is walking in time, learning 'advice from the past'. This remembering is how 'people strive to know events in their entirety, abhorring denials and erasures', like the texture of things in the soil and the way it rearranges itself as he gently turns its layers.

Start again there, in his 'careless body'. This feels like digging, not invasively mining and extracting, but sifting and handling the surface of the place. The twists of iron from a plough and the repaired weave of a fish basket are witness to entangled lives.

/

Huddling there below the road, Herman watches blokes crossing the ford into his pub; they are talking blood again. Perhaps he's starting to let go of the forgetting, as it fizzes like dead cells and husks into that gentle, constant plains breeze   water ribbons an emu drinks   the swamp is refilling.

My words are picking up that remembering, some of which is imaginative.

In the dark, he can hear Mr Pellow's lecture on Australian Missions, droning into the street. Beyond the voice, he may also hear what Reverend Stähle can: the 'silence that descended…after the children had been taken away' from Lake Condah mission.

In *Letters from Aboriginal Women of Victoria, 1867–1926*, the voices of mothers, doubly dispossessed, ring out across this district. He might hear the mail coach carrying those letters, down from the plains and across the stones. He's charged more than once for keeping his boys from school, but it's a small penalty to make sure they stay working on the land.

He petitions for a rail line extension to transport groaning stacks of wheat; then perhaps he remembers black Diggers climbing aboard at the siding as he loads. Some of them come from Framlingham, where families from the former mission fight the Board for the Protection of Aborigines to cultivate land. He extends his property from 1200 to 2000 acres of wheat.

If I can remember, I can see.

See how seeing is made.

See how the vernacular of the Hexham basalt bricks is a homage to the Girrae Wurrung fish runs, 'built of indigenous stone [that] seemed to grow out of the ground'. He is subject to the same desire for settlement: that lushness, the generosity of the volcanic soil; its goodness the creation of a meeting place for neighbours to share; the way 'it becomes increasingly difficult to separate residences...from the activity that sustains the people occupying them'.

See that name, *Weetya*, not as a token of exchange but as a false certificate of ownership.

See how men from nearby nations, forced off the missions, labour with him again at his project of crushing, smoothing and covering.

See how he's driving 'the same roads that took Aboriginal children from their families – firstly on foot, then on horseback, in coaches, trains, and finally in the back of police cars'. Nothing looks the same.

/

I follow the diesel wake of a ute as it cruises the plains. *Justify Your Existence* reads the cabin's rear window, a decal in gothic script.

Rewrite the landscape and the narrative of the selector, the pioneer, the agriculturalist, the ancestor. Embed that small life, entangle it in transnational encounters and unrecorded evidence. As Jan Critchett writes, after collecting oral histories of First Nations lives in the Western District, 'I saw a landscape enriched by new layers of meaning…not part of the experience of the non-Aboriginal community among which the Aboriginals live.' Remember what my myths are made of.

My voice is a proposal: 'the "contact zone" of a shared existence'. Herman is a 'monument to complex histories' that will never be finished because it's made of gaps. This 'proposed monument – the way that the boundary between the monument and the real world is not clear – suggests that there is also no clear line between our lives and our past.'

In this way, he is implied; he's learning how to see deeply. To see lots of scattered things here, through the property he once called mine.

Nan aspires to belong elsewhere, with others.

She might even believe the lies she tells me when I interview her. They are harmless things, really, but together they compose a preferred self.

She is born in 1915, not 1910. Her father is an architect, not a bankrupt carpenter. She is a ladies college student, rather than a seamstress and a housekeeper. She spends visits with her grandparents at Hexham, she isn't left in their care; her mother takes a holiday to Aotearoa once, she doesn't move there for over a decade. Nan has one sister, not several siblings including a half-Māori brother. The surname of her grandfather Herman is… André.

Who you belong with isn't just a name.

In her seventies, Nan is informed by an estranged relative that her half-brother has died. 'I don't have a brother,' is her reply.

When I tell someone about my father's infidelities, often they reply, 'Now you have sisters'. Shocked, the words shoot out of my mouth, a correction of fact. *My father has daughters. I don't have sisters.*

I understand now what my Nan means by her denial, why it isn't merely willful. For us both, a brother or a sister is the name for a quality, an intensity, of relationship. We each grew up with a full, close sibling and that is our measure.

As for her fabrications, I can't say why each of them is necessary for her to make. At some point in her early childhood she is trained not to speak Anders, the German name of her grandparents.

But I can comprehend how important willful denial is to the act of naming oneself, to building the present over the top of the past. Words offer us decisions to make, we must pick them carefully. When we choose one, we rule out others.

The warfront that Robinson finds in the Western District of the Port Phillip colony is already casual, domesticated.

The tracks of livestock are already visible trundling from Lake Bolac towards Portland.

In 1841 he describes the spot, later called Hexham, where my great-great-grandfather Herman Anders will farm some sixty years later.

There, Robinson watches a dog trying to catch an emu
delighted to see the bird streak away
not shot for sport. But in a shepherd's hut one evening
he is shown a double-barreled rifle inlaid with a brass plaque
'from the settlers of Geelong'
to a son who had 'beaten off the natives'.

Tunnerminnerwait has gone ahead of Robinson.

Robinson crosses the Hopkins River
where Nan will later play;
meets what he claims are the worst set of men in the colony
working on one of the big estates.

When I read the names of these estates in his journal, I recognise the ones that proudly feature in the district's historical association and pioneer memorials. I re-read them – listen to the stories behind the names – and I see anti-monuments that spell out unlettered attacks, retaliations, graves. Spell undated wars 1830 to 1859.

Robinson describes the 'pulpy quality' of the marshes around the volcanic stones – they allowed groups of Gunditjmara to run into the stones and escape pursuit during the Eumeralla Wars. He also notices a couple of shepherds guarding flocks, each with a double-barreled rifle. And he notes how a settler stockkeeper, stumbling into Robinson's accommodation, is bleeding from a gash on the back of the neck – by now a familiar injury that represents a reprisal for a settler attack.

When he and Tunnerminnerwait get to Portland on the southern coast, Robinson meets with Henty, the manager of the whaling station where the Convincing Ground massacre had allegedly taken place around 1834. Henty says the name comes from the spot where the whalers fought one another to settle their scores. But Henty has already shared with Robinson information about a massacre, showing a crack in his own denial. He offers to allow Robinson to hear the whalers' oaths. Robinson declines, saying he doesn't trust the whalers to speak the truth.

Speak the truth to whom? I wonder.

Robinson's journals are ignored by the state. They are bureaucratic busywork, proof of a job done.

And yet his journals contain scores of fragments, traces of truth to lob at the White walls of forgetting.

X

Over a hundred and fifty years after Robinson's western travels, at Lake Corangamite Bruce Pascoe locates Colijon, Girrae Wurrung or Djargurd Wurrung fish traps and hut foundations inside an impoverished farmer's boundaries. While there, he also sees how the dry basalt walls of the Western District hark to traditional huts, with 'the stones from destroyed houses…picked up and used to build' new ones by settlers.

The district's lakes are shallow pools set into clean black rings, the water sunk slightly under heavy grass banks. Birds are stuck all over their still surfaces like gravel. Ducks, cygnets, the sky is bulging with early morning cloud after an electrical storm from the coast. Beyond the lakes to the north, I'm looking at the jagged tips of Grampians/Gariwerd, hooked onto the horizon. As the sun climbs and light flushes through the lakelands, what could not be seen a few minutes ago is rising up from the edges and into view.

I buy thick-skinned lemons, borage, eggs and a stem of pigface from a cart beside someone's garden wall. The sky lifts and the pastures appear to stretch. This is where most of the state's butter, cream and cheese is homogenised, pasteurised, loaded onto Sungold and Western Star trucks.

Hayley Millar Baker's pictures of the Western District don't show the invasion of her Gunditjmara ancestors; they show its textures. She is representing her Country as it was and is, at once.

A storm is moving high up, manifest in the swamps as a grey-orange tint, and on the horizon as a swinging, vertical blur of falling rain. Rolling up the coast, the stony rises ripple outward from the old volcanic cones, Tapoc, Mount Napier and Collorrer, Mount Rouse.

The broken base of Rouse is distractingly grand. Grass coverage slips away into some rich depths in the scoria. The peaks were renamed by Major Thomas Mitchell, when he surveyed the central and western grasslands for the first massive pastoral estates in the 1830s.

Millar Baker's work isn't landscape photography. The truth as settlers see it in the present, with the glancing eye, isn't true enough. With digital photomontage she enriches photographic evidence, adding details that have been erased.

Farmhouses are awkwardly built into the uneven hollows, and laval blisters pop through the soil. Everywhere the tumbling, pocked stones and tuff.

By disrupting a photograph's objectivity, Millar Baker can rebuild more accurate narratives. And it was an heirloom – a set of photo negatives from her grandmother – that started her interest in the medium. Her camera may be the coloniser's tool as well as being a matrilineal inheritance; she makes it see what it does because it's both. It's like what Michel Foucault says about the purpose of writing history: 'knowledge is not made for understanding; it's made for cutting'.

As a young woman, maybe Nan visits one of the Scottish estates of the Western District, in the final epoch of its inherited squattocracy. She witnesses the last generation of chatelaines behind loop-holed walls.

/

Walls so thick a heartbeat pauses. The cool of their stone radiates inwards, fills the centre of rooms. In the bar, her Lalique chimes where flanks of Scottie dogs await their tipple. Wind, birdsong of the plains are on mute behind the dining room windows. The lambs eat and eat. Her Spode is green by request. Her butler relinquishes the bathroom by the table when the dinner guests can no longer stagger their way through the parlour.

Her children have already left the district in Japanese cars. They have 'lost touch with wartime sacrifice' and a solid chassis. When her grandchildren visit they ask silly questions about the name on the gates.

She is always looking out: to her other interior, the basalt enclosure. To that 'security of tenure with no armed invaders'. She is always remembering the clan tree in the library, never forgetting the swatch of tartan that recalls the highland clearances.

In the smoking room she keeps her trinkets. Iron Age spearheads and ivory fans, a drinking horn and tiny birds' nests, dried sponges and her mother of pearl, the blue ducks. One day 'foreign raiders' with 'Chinese or Arab names' will take them all.

'To own land in the Western District was to rule.' Her hats hang as still as the landscapes over the mantle, faded and water-damaged by south-west skies.

On the wetland reserved for game, the swans honk their demands.

/

In tweaking her own class towards the grandchildren of squatters, Nan must think that their culture is alive. Instead, she's witnessing a dying race, the last of a tribe. They will become the stuff of museums.

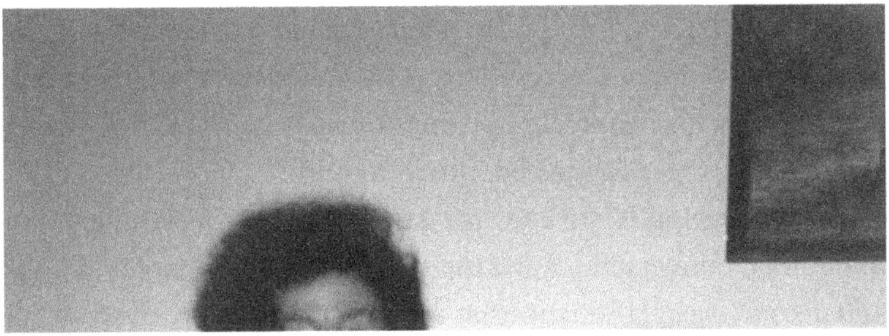

I'm in my underwear again, cross-legged on another chenille bedspread. This room's pretty good: spacious enough for a bag to spew its contents, a countertop for takeaway containers and kettle, a TV with clear reception of *Antiques Roadshow*. Hot, strong showerhead. Clean, large bed. Quiet car park.

In the evening, I sit like this and write up everything I can remember. Conversations and interviews, descriptions of buildings and people, casual thoughts that echo through the day, even what I ate. It's a way of remembering tiny things that might otherwise get lost, things that might later reveal themselves as big; and it's also a way to process what I've seen or heard. Remembering is deliberate, after all; it's a series of decisions.

If I wake in an inland town, it's too early for business. I'm back onto the bitumen without coffee or conversation. I watch the sunrise over long, flat plains or marshes covered in birds.

In big towns and cities, I'm straight to the public library, past commuters with other things on their minds. I get the protocols of archives all wrong; neglecting to locker my bag or realising that I've come with my forbidden phone-camera rather than a pencil. I'm anxious about whether all the items I've ordered have been brought out by the librarians; there were so many I requested a week ago that I've lost track of them all. Seven or eight times out of ten, I go through the items on the trolley – land deeds, wills, photo folders – quickly.

Every page or image needs to be checked, even briefly – there might be one word or place name that lights up. Time recedes and I linger with this one, noting all sorts of minutiae *just in case*. Because I've only got this one day set aside for this collection, I won't be able to access this again in a hurry. It's not digitised. It's not duplicated.

Across the wooden tables, a pair of women is looking at public records for genealogical information – like me, except I'm envious that they have personal letters and I've a dispute over some unpaid invoices for sheep. I'm enjoying the waves of excitement they're putting out, heads close together, stifling gasps. They are completely compelled by their own emotional investment in these barely known people. It's beautiful. But as the gasps continue and they begin talking at normal volume, reciting phrases aloud, I'm getting annoyed. I haven't got long in this air-conditioned bunker, just me and the documents, and I can't concentrate. I can't get lost in it like they are. After I've gone through the trolley and returned to the street with all its distractions, I'm slightly resentful at cheating myself of immersion in other lives.

In the dusk I walk along the sprawling, abandoned streets to a pub set gorgeously on a bend in a creek. I get in before any locals have even thought about drinks or dinner, so there's an hour of free wifi and sour Riesling. It's mid-winter, I dib the couch beside the open fire. An hour must have passed because I'm suddenly aware of voices filling the room and the gentle clink of pint glasses.

No one's joined my spot by the fire yet, but in another hour, two women ask if they can sit opposite. I eavesdrop on their entire conversation while eating defrosted calamari. They are golfers, planning a tour. They're late-fifties, impressively slim and fit. They call out greetings to other groups walking in. The room is starting to swell with voices, it's become dark outside. As I finish eating, I hear one of the older, fair-skinned drinkers behind me calling out to the bartender.

Did he say

I turn and see a young man with a heavy black beard behind the bar. But am I really listening?

They know each other, I remind myself. I'm the outsider, here, don't make assumptions. There are no double-barreled rifles on the wall. No one is bleeding.

The bartender makes a blunt, sarcastic reply. I don't know if I heard right.

Or am I carrying something in my ears, something not remembered but uncovered? Time to call it a night and, tipsy under the sodium-lit streets of the main drag, return to my rented bed.

The Stars

Wimmera Mallee, Victoria
(1860–1920)

'Another Wimmera girl!' says Kat.

'Well, I didn't grow up there,' I answer sheepishly.

Kat is a Wotjobaluk woman. A writer and curator, she's doing research into a deep ancestry. She plans to travel to Germany and access records of Moravian missionaries who came to her Country in the 1840s.

I ask Kat to help me pronounce some local names. I realise that my Nan's grandfather, Herman Anders would have known them, or at least heard them spoken. Eventually they would have become more familiar to him than his native language.

Since Nan didn't say or didn't know about his life before Hexham, I'm going to follow him backwards. Because before he chooses Hexham, he toils in the Wimmera Mallee forty years. He got there on foot from South Australia. Herman, his brother and father landing in Adelaide in 1856 from Crossen an der Öder, then a town at the eastern boundary of the Prussian Empire. When they departed Europe they were cobblers; now they are looking for fertile soil to steal.

Kat asks me if I have heirlooms.

'No,' I answer, wondering.

From the native-pine huts of Murtoa, the cobbler's son looks back, southward. He can still just discern an indigo possibility on that horizon. It pulses there, flexing its peaks of granite and greenstone all the way down to the bank buildings of Hamilton. It's not the ocean but the range has a similar, magnetic orientation.

That southern range, the old Irish shepherds tell him, is good for grazing and the rain shadows that spin around its jagged outcrops.

They have sheltered in its overhangs painted with child-sized hands. These fellows are the ones who pointed his family towards Murtoa, who seem glitched by something faraway and very near, who whisper to him of the large man who sits in a cave adjacent the range with his dog, glowing.

To the east is the deep depression of Lake Buloke and its banks of cleared mounds and dunes. The cobbler's son is looking for a place to cultivate but it's too constrained in Murtoa, in this cluster of his countrymen. Life is Prussian, sometimes. Once again, they find themselves on the fringe of an expanding state. Except here there is no centre, no guard, no emblem.

He's not alone or lonely; he travels away with his wife and father, and baby. Driving the bullocks north, sometimes they stay with a tent while he rides ahead with the dray full of tools, through gnarled groves of black-trunked buloke and mallee gum. The earth is rose-pink.

Weeks after talking to Kat, I remember. There are two heirlooms.

One of them is the locket of Herman's youngest daughter, Emily; my great-grandmother. She died young and I've often imagined the locket on her pale chest as she lay in bed and said goodbye to her children. It went to one of her daughters, Nan. When she died, my mother gave it to me.

The Wimmera Mallee region undulates across the north-west quadrant of Victoria, 'all red, tussocky ground'. Some call it back country, but then there would have to be a front. The cobbler's son no longer has a sense of water nearby; it feels landlocked, and yet there are rivers and creeks gently feeding the plains. There are lakes, they say.

He's following the Yarriambiack Creek, a pathway engrained in the earth and moving beside him. Swaggies show him a route northward to the squatter's run, the route that was shown to them by the Wotjobaluk. It sets off from the ancient campsite by the swamp at Murtoa. From time to time, he's seen the Wotjobaluk families walking in this direction. The German-speaking kids trail along with them for a mile or so, chatting. Eventually the Wotjobaluk parents will send the town kids back to their homes.

When his nephews come in after dusk, they tell him Wergaia names that run into his ears like water.

I can't locate the centre of Murtoa. A divvy van cruises the empty streets, it's mid-afternoon on a Wednesday. Sometimes after February westerlies, back at home I find this dust on my decking.

The cobbler's son and his family follow the steps of others in the soft soil, wheel ruts and boot tracks that stay in print for weeks. They haven't thought to ask permission; that opportunity was buried with the squatters before them.

As their horses navigate the creek banks, the 'signs of early native occupation increase until Lake Corrong is reached'. A trail of prior settlement that will lead them to the chain of lakes fed by the Wimmera River. From time to time their path is crossed by young Wergaia men and couples travelling from the mission, eastwards to visit relatives, seasonal work, or proper rations elsewhere.

The highway sticks close to the Yarriambiack Creek all the way from Warracknabeal to Beulah, Rosebery and Hopetoun. The creek is a busy, dense borderland at the edge of wide fertilised paddocks.

At Warracknabeal, they find the creek is fat with the last shower. A few emus circle about a broad, trodden part of the bank. Redgums lean in. Some have oblongs excised from their bark. The flat rectangles under the bark look like closed doors. When he sees huge teal eggs amongst the grass he backs out of the clearing, through the bright trunks.

These months are spent in tents, his wife and baby daughter are always close to the ground.

The creek begins to empty into winding corridors of dusty ironbark and blackwood. Frogs roar through the nights. There are crabholes but scarce water.

I feel closer to Herman's family, here, in the light and shade.

At Warracknabeal, posters promote mental health counselling for families. Emus stroll along the creek within a fenced enclosure. The town's roundabouts sport bronze monuments to wheat and grazing, patrolled by bronze dingoes.

Dingoes and wild dogs are hunted relentlessly by Herman and his neighbours. But, warns the Western Vermin Commission in 1893, 'a wild dog could not always be distinguished from a tame dog which had gone wild'.

Boundaries are easy to draw but hard to patrol. The wheat's in bronze, but not the murnong and laarp harvesting that the squatters' kids see.

Lake Corrong is a scrubby and damp depression. Cattle and sheep wander through the boggy middle of it.

The cobbler's son and the cobbler go to work for the owner of this vast lease, like everyone else. The owner offers loans and stores to settlers who are buying their own allotments and employs men from the mission and creek camps to join the station on shearing and bark-stripping for a couple of weeks.

The one who works here the longest is Jowley, a shearer and drover who began living in the homestead as a boy. 'The Last Aborigine of Lake Corrong,' says the station owner, almost proudly.

Jowley says he was an infant at the time of the 'big fight'.

Jowley lists the names of groups that came to meet, trade and camp at the lake when it was full. And soon enough the cobbler's son sees for himself that some of those people are still coming and going.

Jowley lives in his own place these days, and sometimes at a hut on the creek, and sometimes at the mission. He's too old to walk as far as he used to; but when the cobbler's son and the cobbler tell Jowley where they've journeyed from, he recounts their path from Murtoa in reverse and further, west across the border into South Australia.

The Lake Corrong station eventually forms the town of Hopetoun. In the centre of Hopetoun, a freestanding board depicts the settlement's founder, Peter McGinnis, surrounded by his family. At the edge of the family group stands the Yarrikaluk boy, Jowley, in an Edwardian suit with a cute lizard protruding from his pocket.

One local history source says that two Yarrikaluk bands slaughtered one another at Lake Corrong. Another says that 'at some stage' the McGinnis family 'were joined' by Jowley. It also says that the station hands once 'gave chase' to a Yarrikaluk group that took some flour; in that group was Jowley's mother, who placed her baby in a hollow and 'would have been too frightened to come and claim him'. Later Jowley is sometimes called 'black Peter

McGinnis', as though he's the shadow of the squatter; as though he doesn't have a name or a family.

The days are long, in summer they barely end. Conversations are truncated before the lamps are turned down into deep, short sleep. While the cobbler's son and his family lie unconscious, a pair of curlews calls across the darkness. The birds remember where water would return, where lakes would come.

There are several children in the house now and on Sundays, once a month, the whole family attends a service held at the station. Jowley and his wife go over to the mission. The cobbler's son and his family have never seen the Moravian mission, it's not open for public viewing like the other institutions. This year, for the first time, there's a Christmas appeal for the mission children. Maybe the cobbler gives money or toys because the eroded earth has covered his tracks with sand.

The earth gives the cobbler's son more than he can use. On one side of the lake is a raised bank, a lip that cops the wind. He's tasked with clearing the bulokes, and then pressing down the sandy mounds to avoid erosion. Before the cleared hills are flattened, though, the wind gets into them and brushes the loosened sand from a pair of skeletons.

   A local newspaper office puts the bones on display. While folks come and stare at them, the cobbler's son carries on digging catchments across the run. Above, a constantly tumbling sky carries water to the south and east. Nearly everyday his hands and tools come into contact with domestic scenes, burials or shallow graves.

He crushes the scrub with a log roller pulled by six bullocks, burns off the leftovers, and then ploughs through the hidden mallee roots. As the last of the lake's water dries away, he touches mussel shells, smithereens of emu eggs, stone implements, broken millstones, hammer stones.

He saves a few bright things, but there's nowhere to put the rest so he pushes it down, further into his livelihood.

Near the town's picture of the founding family, I find the busy mural that Hopetoun includes on all its tourist material. A panorama, its figures sit on multiple picture planes, different eras appear to be living simultaneously. They are contained by the wall; when it runs out, so does time and space.

He's worked out that the best blocks run between the creek and the lake. Clay soil, fairly grassed. He buys three allotments down near Jowley's place, and together they build a small stone hut for the cobbler's son and his family.

Newspapers publish reports of burials uncovered all over the Mallee, from rabbiters and selectors in the west at Edenhope, up to the Murray River, and down to Mokepilly.

At the far left of the mural, a portrait of Jowley as an old man floats beside two Wotjobaluk hunters chasing kangaroo. They are separate scenes but seem to be joined together, as a kind of prologue to the rest of the mural. Then, and now. Or you could read the mural from foreground to horizon line: cattle drovers, wheat stookers and a lone swagman are all walking away from me, to the top of the wall. Here, and there.

All of them are White although many of them, not just Jowley, were Wotjobaluk. Where are they going? I want to ask the artist. Is it into a different version of the past, over that line? Or are the White drovers moving into the land of forgetting?

When the cobbler's son first started working the Wimmera Mallee he considered showing Jowley his pocketful of blades and beads, but he gave them to his small daughter, Emily, instead. When she toddled out to the station carrying lunch for her father and brothers, some kindness helped her to get along. He guessed at the meaning of the objects for her, scratching the air with the serrated stone.

Occasionally, on a late autumn night, Jowley's wife comes by the house of the cobbler's son and smokes beside the fire to warm up. William, the eldest boy, asks to try her pipe. He asks if it's true that her sons are champion runners now. He used to meet the Wotjobaluk teenagers who worked on the station but they haven't left the mission in a long while.

At the back of Hopetoun, I come across a lone kangaroo dog, quivering in the road. She looks through me and stalks away down the street, which leads into a pasture clear to the horizon.

One day, he drives the new plough over the top of the history he never really learned. Because the vast middens of this knowledge keep coming and he cannot read it any longer, he's exhausted to sift this technology and touch the bones of the hands that touched it.

   But even after he has left the Wimmera Mallee, pursuing easier soil, still he will open the newspaper or his door and hear from sightseers who go out collecting at the lakes. It's a tide of human settlement that flows into and through his life. When the bullocks are spent he flogs his horses to plough until he's charged for cruelty.

When the cobbler's son sets out of the house early in the morning, Jowley is walking from his hut along the creek to the station homestead, carrying a waddy all the way. Sometimes his wife is there with her gun. They bag up the rabbits. When the whirl of dust travels up from the south, carrying the inspector, they stay down at the creek for a few days.

Lake Lascelles, created as a reliable water source for the settler farmers, is kept pumped with water below the town of Hopetoun. Now it's a pleasure place for campers, and tradies having a quiet lunch. It sparkles painfully in the sun, and then ruffles and laps under the wind.

At the end of our conversation, Kat advises me on the proper way to approach and leave a site where bad spirits might dwell. They come up from the ground, through the feet, she explains.

When it does fall onto the Wimmera Mallee region, the rain is channeled across the allotments. Lake Corrong remains empty. The older local stockmen say the lakes had been dry like this before the whitefellas came. The cobbler's son disagrees. He says there are too many weirs on the feeding river, the Wimmera, the rainwater can barely collect before it's siphoned into the big pastoralist's tanks. The farmers need enough for wheat, oats and a few sheep at least. So fallowing is the way, he feels, that 'cleans the land and keeps it...in good heart'.

I don't know if Herman recognises the land was being ruined, or if he thinks it is poor country in need of improvement, or if he understands that a lake or a river can go underground until it's needed on the surface. He probably doesn't understand that he is drawing up old water from the aquifer, and that it will take years to replenish.

Beside the filled lake is another mural. I recognise the image of Bunjil creating Grampians/Gariwerd, and his blazing daughter Karakarooc. There's Tchingal, the giant emu whose death near Horsham is a reminder of the cycle of drought and flood.

The railway approaches. Lake Corrong is almost entirely divided into allotments to encourage settlement. He buys up more, creating a block from the creek to the main road by the cemetery. He becomes occupied with breaking down large, oily mounds of singed rocks, the ovens that the old station owner warned him about. He digs more channels into his lease. He rotates the crops and he fallows. The rain doesn't come.

The long-burning mallee roots are smoking over the emptied plains. He watches things rising through the ploughed earth.

The youngest of Herman's children, Emily will be the first in her family to imagine the owners of the land out of sight.

The earth gets drier, men get thirstier and their work runs thin. He looks back the way he came.

The street that follows the creek that joins the old campsites, that joins the impressions of water bodies. The cobbler's son names the street for himself and his father. Then he builds a hotel beside his family's house and names it Rosebery. He builds a hotel and names it Rosebery, south of the old meeting place that Jowley described. He builds a hotel and names it Rosebery, south of the old meeting place that Jowley described, and north of the old campsite on the edge of Warracknabeal. He names the street for himself.

There's business to be found in others' despair; another kind of fallowing. Single men must drink somewhere, talk and sometimes sleep. The cobbler's son charters a coach down to Warracknabeal to bring more travellers to his hotel. Most of them have been turfed out of the bigger town earlier in the night, fighting their way out of the carriage and into Rosebery. It's the indigo hour, the first stars are playing through the pepper trees he has planted outside the hotel. The cook sharpens her knife.

Around the back of Herman Anders's pub, my eye is caught by a shiny Australian flag, polyester blue, crumpled in the grass like a sleeping animal.

Emily is four when she attends the tiny funeral of her grandfather the cobbler, 'the first burial' in Rosebery. She fingers the fence around the neat mound of pink earth. These are the limits of her world. People come into it or go out. This mound is what she sees when she thinks about the soil that grew her.

Her father, the cobbler's son, is knocked out by a drunk. The scar heals into a pale dent like a tiny dry lake on his temple, as he watches the railway extend parallel to his street. At last, the train stops opposite his hotel door. Indian hawkers camp in town with their cargo of vegetables, pans and dynamite. A passing shower, credit replaces cash.

The more cleared plains, the more constant the wind. If you stop moving, it catches up. If you lie down, you'll get buried.

Amongst the bulokes along the creek, it sways softly.

The cook tries to cut her own throat. 'Her injuries are not serious,' the cobbler's son tells the journalist from Horsham. His wife drives the girl to town for a doctor, and then to the local magistrate to explain herself. The cook refuses to promise that she won't try again. She has conversations on this trip that will never be recorded or overheard.

By the time she's twelve and walking back home from the school next door, Emily's collection of Wotjobaluk tools surround her bed in the corner of the back verandah. This is the yield she takes from the Wimmera Mallee. A dying world of lost people, *reads her mother from the paper after supper. The child wields the heavy iron over the family's clothes embedded with soil.*

The air around the remains of Rosebery is dented. My photo of the pub's ruins comes out as a grey blur – the close-up of a tin can, a dirty sheet, or the edge of a storm. The haze that my great-grandmother Emily sees when she imagines a dying race.

Her locket is a pink gold disc with a hidden spring catch. It has a machine-turned design, a series of infinite spirals, worked into the metal. Inside is a yellowed silk lining covered by a concave glass lens. It's empty when my mother gives it to me.

I'm often afraid to wear it, in case the tiny barrel clasp should open and the whole thing tumble down my chest, and away. So instead I look into the empty glass, the fish-eye reflection, and through it to the slip of lining. That window, maybe some red dust still stuck under its rim, is a memento of what might be.

More wind comes over the rolled plains and the heads of so many disappointed men. The rabbits have dug in and they will never be extricated. Mick, James, Babar and Kurt have hanged themselves in this ten years at Rosebery. He's lucky to have a family, then. Or is it something else that drives him in straight lines.

The cobbler's son leads a petition to the state, to pay settlers for relief work digging channels. He dictates the letters to his wife, her hand is steadier and she softens the nicks in his grammar. He continues to rotate the fields every three years, he intones, because 'the old slovenly, slapdash style of cultivation had to be abandoned'.

There must be no more 'squeezing'. The earth here 'cracks very freely' he pumps his hand open and shut, and must be 'scarified' to hold in the winter moisture. The earth has been drying for years, he doesn't say. Let the old tree breaks stand and hold onto the soil, he doesn't say. Instead, 'I believe in the fertility of the soil' and his wife knows he's telling the truth. 'I have given the Mallee a thorough trial' as though it had to defend itself.

Once, the monument to the people of the Wimmera Mallee was a clean plough. It's now been joined by other signs. Up and down the highway, wheat silos by the railway are painted with giant portraits of locals. They make small lives epic in scale, men and women, young and old.

On one of them, Wotjobaluk elders and children are painted before a starry plains sky. National Trust has handed the former Ebenezer mission site down at Dimboola back to its traditional owners. Locked safely against free access, its buildings take their place beside a burial ground and an ancient meeting site, held by the community.

Someone in the pub says that the remains of Jowley's father have been found by a swaggie up near the lake by the station. There are signs of injury to the skull.

The cobbler's son feels it in himself – the nearness of his own father underground. He wants to ask Jowley about that big fight, and maybe he does. He'd like Emily to know but the girl has gone off to teach in the school next door.

For the Rosebery class of 1899 Emily has written a play, 'The Dying World', to rehearse for the solstice pageant.

Herman will outlive his daughter, Emily. He and Eliza will help to raise her girls. But by then he'll have turned away from the Wimmera Mallee, to the rich soils of the Western District. What will he tell those girls about Lake Corrong? And what won't he tell?

He probably doesn't know that it's settled deeply in his cells, even though his body hurts from the labour required to flatten it down. It's not crushed or burned. It flashes like the ring on a closed fist. It's in the unburied hoard, dusted with vermillion soil, that he put into his daughter's hands.

Rosebery is a ghost town where settlers go to haunt themselves.

There's still hope for the Mallee, the cobbler's son says aloud. The clouds keep passing like bundles of seed-heads: a deluge that takes shape, hovers, and then moves over the southern horizon.

He sells the pub and the allotment titles. Once again, he flees the fringe when it begins to rip.

Eliza and the children take the train to Ararat, gliding over the ground, almost immediately unaware of where they are. He prepares the bullocks to follow the road beside the creek back to its source.

He goes to see Jowley and his wife, and maybe he leaves something with them. Behind him, those who were here before. They will still be there long after his grandchildren die. Behind him, his detritus – a cluster of bricks and pepper trees, piles of glass bottles, mounded graves.

Emily's locket is delicate, fashionable but modest, and made to last – to frame a choice.

When she grows up, she'll go away – first to the farm at Hexham, and then to Aotearoa with her husband. But she will return to the Wimmera Mallee, to die at thirty-five. Her father the cobbler's son, and her daughter Nan, will watch her go back into that pink soil.

The second heirloom is Herman's bullock bell. Throughout my childhood it hung by the front door of our home in Cronulla, where it was the sound – that flat din on rough iron – that a guest had arrived.

Can I talk of a settler family's forgetting as a cumulative condition? The hardening of millions of soft denials into unknowing?

A few things removed by each generation, initially unnoticed.

It starts with pacification of the body. To make a future for their kids, Herman Anders and his wife Eliza need to be able to wash off that Wimmera Mallee dust.

Their daughter, my great-grandmother Emily, has it cleaned from her eyes. She is among the first to see only block colours of brown, green and blue.

Suppose it doesn't work; we know that forgetting and denial are different functions of the brain.

The gothic nature of pioneer fictions, a land haunted by colonial violence or appropriated beliefs, perpetuate the idea that the past only comes to visit people – that it dwells elsewhere, in another dimension, or that it comes and goes from the land in the form of a spectre. But, says Tony Birch, 'country is not interested in some white person's melancholia or their sense of being haunted…land has inherent rights and an inherent sense of dignity that doesn't require those superficial narratives to give it meaning'.

The violence of Herman's pastoralism lives within him, not within the Wimmera Mallee. My husband suggests I should make Herman nastier, more brutish in his determination to trample those rights and dignity: he sees them *and* he tramples them. The harsh toll of the bullock bull sets the tone, as if the charm pressed into the iron wasn't enough: *SUCCESS TO BULLOCK DRIVERS*. But I feel it is all much more subconscious than that.

I could make his wife Eliza more waspish, less tolerant of her fringe society, and more controlling of little Emily. And if I do, the responsibility for it will be on me who tells the story detached from memory, not on the ground that sustains their family.

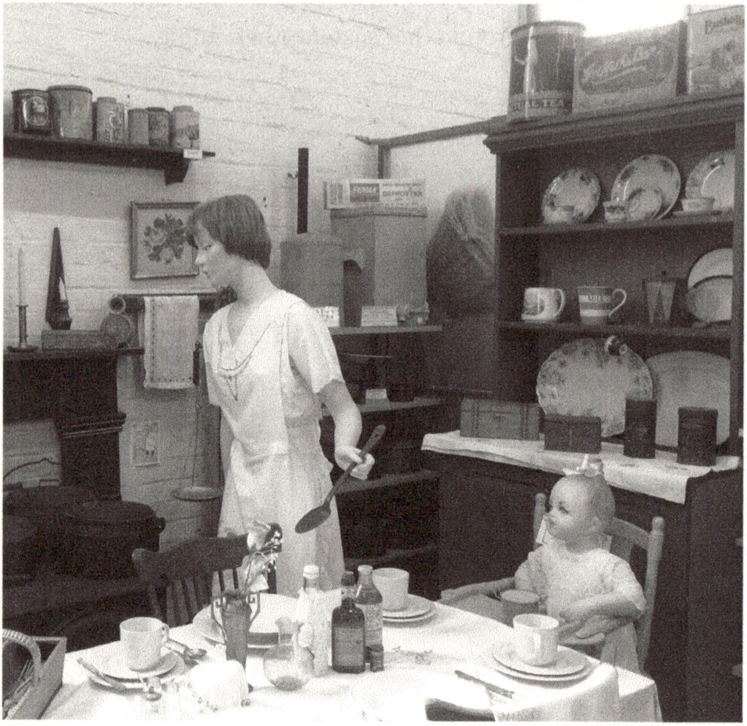

'The memory, monuments and memorials...will be all around you'.

Just outside Ararat, in some of the old grazing properties under Langi Ghiran, big twisted redgums have been left standing amongst small groves of grass. The pastures look lightly stocked. This is near the headwaters of the Hopkins River that runs down to Hexham, then onwards into the Southern Ocean at Warrnambool.

One of the largest trees bares open its broad trunk, containing a small room. I meet a Gunditjmara man who describes this grove as 'a very old hospital'.

The fight to divert a highway development away from the trees has been long and exhausting for their custodians, the Djab Wurrung. Later, I hear that one of these sacred trees has been felled. My husband forwards me a photo that somebody has sent him from the main street of Ararat. It shows a dump truck carrying the gigantic stump of the tree.

They're parading the dead tree through town says the photographer's caption.

The threat of the highway development isn't contained to the gnarled, bulbous redgums – the Djab Wurrung say it's a network of tradition and kinship that stretches out between and around the trees. Djab Wurrung woman and Senator Lidia Thorpe describes the trees as 'deeply intimate cultural sites, which literally contain the blood of Aboriginal women, giving these trees nutrients to grow for so long'.

X

Ararat's local history society resides in a chilly former woolstore off the main drag. It's filled with aisles of vitrines and shelves. A mannequin in an apron tends a blonde baby doll and a meat safe, beside a case of Martini-Henry rifles donated from nearby properties.

The museum boasts the largest collection of First Nations artefacts in Victoria.

During the twentieth century, amateur collectors disturb more evidence of First Nations history in Victoria than the plough. Ararat vigneron Laurence Mooney collects and donates a startling range of tools and objects to the museum. Most are from north and western regions of Australia, but a few items – a shield, a boomerang and a coolamon – are local to the Hopkins River area.

Beside Mooney's donation, another case contains artefacts 'bequeathed to Ararat' by Charles Best. On one of the shelves sits a Victorian portrait of a local First Nations woman in a crinoline and cap. Below her, a wooden miniature boat – crafted for a First Nations boy who dwelled with a local squatter, having 'become separated from his parents'.

I hear my own desolate footfalls on the creaking floorboards as the contents of glass cases rattle in my wake.

In western Victoria, some amateur collectors have kept their artefact collections secret out of fear about land claims. I'm told of a landowner who still refuses to repatriate remains because of this misunderstanding.

Some public institutions make repatriation a core concern; others want to control the lives of objects. Only twenty years ago, Gary Foley and the Dja Dja Wurrung try to exercise the right to permanently hold some barks that are on loan from the British Museum. 'When does a spear that isn't thrown cease to be a spear, and become a mere stick?' asks Dja Dja Wurrung academic Tiriki Onus. The British Museum refuses repatriation, and the Melbourne Museum launches a case against the Dja Dja Wurrung.

The Mooney and Best collections are mementos – evidence of settlers' own continuity. Shared as public heritage they're symbols of the past that act as visible, tangible props to our narratives of inheritance and permanence.

And yet, Lidia Thorpe questions the effects of erasing such monuments to colonisation. Perhaps they have an ongoing purpose. 'There is a big story to be told,' the senator says. 'Let's tell the whole story and we will all learn something from it.'

Counter-narratives to whitewashing in Australia are invented by First Nations people. They start like cracks within colonists' documents, and quickly move into the form of letters, then petitions. They are embodied in the historical record of walk-offs and songs, witness statements, rallying speeches and novels, artworks; records that anyone may access. Memorials that anyone may visit.

/

Whitewashing of Wimmera Mallee pioneer life has ignored the disenfranchisement and violation of First Nations lives: and by the same principle it also skims over the heart-, mind- and body-breaking experiences of its very own hero, the freeholding settler. 'With the flattening of trees a people's collective soul is scarified.'

Herman Anders mullenises the mallee scrub up in Wotjobaluk Country, handles its knowledge and technology, its remains from ancient campsites and burials. He has a lot of time to consider this: his haphazard farming project is laboured, slowed by the history and ecology of the land before him. It is perverse in its difficulty, persisting in the Wimmera Mallee despite 'the baffling density of semi-arid woodland, the jarring roots' that repulse clearance.

It's not possible to handle the earth daily and simply fail to notice its intricacies, delights, its insistence. Since I first visited the Wimmera Mallee I've moved to a place where my eyes and hands are regularly close to the ground around my home, where even daily firewood collection brings me into contact with the complexities of soil, roots, limbs. My point is, it takes a forceful act upon oneself to ignore this domestic, intimate wealth of purposeful life.

Truth-telling means acknowledging that this flattening was felt by individuals and families, not by collectives of towns or states or a nation. If I repeat stories about a hostile land that either punishes the pioneer or is dominated by them, I don't consider the relationships of their soul.

To *quit* a region, like Herman Anders quit the Wimmera Mallee, is a euphemism as emotionally opaque as *taking up land*. What is felt when a settler leaves the toxic society they have normalised or the soil they have abused for decades? What do they miss, regret, or relieve?

And if I repeat those mythic stories here in the museum, I don't notice that the mannequin's hands aren't rubbed raw from the mangle propped beside her, or that there aren't any flies humping on the meatsafe. The embodied reading of a place has its purposes, but truth-telling demands factual accuracy as well.

Before me, under glass, my great-grandmother Emily Anders' name is inscribed on a reproduction of Charles Nuttall's *The Opening, Commonwealth Parliament*. This monument to Federation is presented as a citizens' gift to the Ararat Council in 1907.

The forgetting has been done for her, too. She doesn't have her father Herman's accent, and she hasn't encountered the generation of murderers amongst the stockmen and shepherds he'd found when he arrived. She is part of a generation of 'Australian natives', as they call themselves, disconnecting from European origins and fusing local history into stories of self-made time and place.

I could make Emily conservative. I could make her, now a twenty-year-old fiancée, cross the street in Ararat to avoid someone a shade too dark. I could make her write a letter to the protectorate, to request a girl who might be capable of nannying her daughters. Who will prove me wrong? Am I poisoning the writing of history?

A year after having her name inscribed on this gift, though, she and her husband move to Aotearoa. For fourteen years, she dwells there. Emily has time to become a guest in another language, terrain, culture, history – and colony – on the east coast of the North Island. It seems she leaves behind her daughters, Nan and her sister, with her parents in the Western District. What does she take with her?

Maybe, deep down she carries a knowledge that the people of the Wimmera Mallee 'shared the same air, heard the same sounds and walked in each other's footsteps'.

I leave the museum, the doorbell jangling into the space of disembodied things.

Pieces of the bridge float by, rushing to the river-mouth and then, like a change of mind, bobbing back past her feet as the tide heaves in.

Her tits ache. The newest baby, born here, hangs from her like a dragging anchor.

The landing bell clangs and she turns to face the Pacific – a soft line that is buckling into the brute form of a steamer. Down on the flats, a train of bullocks is already being steered towards the shore, deeper into the flooded mix of earth and sand.

Emily is twenty-nine.

The sound and sight – bell and bullock – make a fast tapping inside her, beneath the baby. And though she's turned away from it, other things remind of that rough Wimmera Mallee time: the wayfarers passing through, the drinkers of a night, the suicides, the swell of the population at threshing, the men who work in their sleep. The men who leave for days. A sense of standing at the edge.

Of what? A shipyard crew is moving about the bullocks and tugboats in the shallow swell. Emily's mind calls them native, half-caste, and British, but they are indistinguishable from that distance. They are overseen by old Wiremu, at his own appointment. In fact, excepting her husband, they are all well over middle-aged. Every able man under sixty from around East Cape has enlisted – plenty of them from the iwi, too.

Emily works on her shame like a torn skirt that needs mending. She throws it in the Uawa. Nearly ten years ago she saw the brilliant Federation memorial hanging in the Ararat town hall with her name inscribed. Now, she would enlist herself if she could. And she'd happily defend New Zealand. They've refused Chinese and Arabs. If her father lived here, he'd be slapped in the street for muttering German. The river breathes out and in.

For all the pamphlets on British purity that the tourists leave in the train carriages or pick up at a Sunday service, though, Emily has never seen so many brown bodies. They talk their lingo when they come through town, and then are quoted by the newspapers speaking Queen's English in Parliament. The back blocks of Tolaga Bay they lease from Whites, the bright clapboard church is their own devising, yet they are constantly organising to ask for more land. It has taken her the first year or two here to discover that there is no longer any mission.

Sea-purple eyes of a *marae* blink from a low rise on the Uawa's south bank. Above them a mountain of sea-floor, green as the fish hooks around the shiphands' necks.

As the mountain of greenstone above Hexham, back in Victoria. Her infant girls are there; and here, in the locket like a hot swelling on her collarbone.

She thinks of them on the blown plains, grass to their waists, hearing the harsh of cypress softly breaking under its own weight. Building tiny heaps of basalt pebbles in their grandfather's paddocks.

It isn't just a matter of colour. Her husband's brat up at the native village has turned five. It can ask for its father. Soon it will be able to find its way down from the hills, to him. Its mother sends Emily a gift, a woven bag, which she hides in a drawer.

Emily picks a path away from the ocean, above the flood wrack. She saw the ocean once before she met her fiancé and sailed away: Eliza drove the carriage to Warrnambool, following the Hopkins down as it pulsed stronger and stronger then cascaded into the saltwater like fingerlings. The salt-drenched vegetation grew flamboyant, as it does here. Her girls might see the ocean, too, if her father has business there.

She reaches the steep track up to the Pakarae Hotel. With its view over the headland, the broken bridge, it is like a boat marooned. When her husband takes off to the woman's village overnight, she mans the telephone station tacked onto the back of the hotel. The job is supposed to be his exemption from enlistment. Her boys scream unchecked in the hotel garden as she manages the switchboard. All its busy knobs and lights look to Emily like the wives of Tolaga Bay, talking talking.

When the boys go quiet it means the kids from the back blocks have come on their horses to fish, snagging hers along the way.

Emily likes the very old Māori men and women. Their blackened lips and chins held proudly like carved busts, she thinks. They leave the town to itself, even old Wiremu returns to the hinterland before sunset. But their young people and children are devious and bold. Not like the natives at home, who'd wait until they were spoken to.

Tolaga Bay's housewives and farmers keep White society neat as a mantlepiece, but this coast is checked by another law.

Like soil into sand, she's been folded into it before she knows.

Her girls in Hexham are saved from it all.

Threshold

Goldfields, Central Victoria
(1850–2022)

Me
| | | |
―――
|
My mother –
| |
―――
|
My mother's father – Nan
|
―――
|
My mother's grandmother – My mother's grandfather
| |
―――   ―――
| |
Bessie Lynn –   Alice Cleburne – Henry Curwen-Walker
| | | | | |
―――   ―――   ―――

Adam Loftus Lynn – Marianne Ferres   Richard Cleburne   John Curwen-Walker

phalaris goes between tussocks gripping big hunks of soil, fixed

but thistle bothers me most it fights back tall personal.
a full bucket of it wacks   i'm looking forward
to watching it burn, blinking the haze.
i excel at plucking the thing that grows again.
thorns scotch my wrists through the gloves.
milk snaps out the root stays in the earth.
i'm holding the head aloft like a prize
accidentally given to the wrong poet. i'm axing the mattock.

thistle and phalaris show in rashes under the cherry ballart,
let herbicide sap
reply to fire biting the ground cleared.

guests never leave.
on a sheep station in the western district
pulling them by hand from the grasslands
reserve i would like to shoot
thistle and phalaris inside the walled garden.

X

i know i'm entering wathaurong when farmers have stacked
red boulders in paddock corners like dust sweepings.
and i see when the basalt keeps rising
under the crops decade after century
but never exhausted the soil flies away
the stones stay.

Tom Nicholson is a monument-maker. Only, no sooner are his monuments glimpsed, than they're packed away. Nicholson treads lightly. He cuts traces in the mind.

Nicholson first made *Towards a monument to Batman's Treaty* in 2013. It reappeared over seven years in slightly different forms and locations. It is perpetually provisional.

Until quite recently, John Batman was named a founder of Melbourne. A squatter in Van Diemen's Land, he had already stolen Maulboyheener's infant brother. In 1835 he tries to annex Port Phillip and extend his grazing. He creates his own document to purchase the land directly from the leaders of the Wurundjeri, traditional owners of Narrm, Melbourne.

As a private contract for so-called British land his agreement is declared void by the state. (The state's own legal right to the land was, of course, also void.) But Batman's so-called 'treaty' is considered a false deal in other ways, since few can believe that Batman grasps the Wurundjeri's terms or that he makes his intentions properly clear to them: permanent and total land use on the Merri Merri Creek in exchange for an annual quantity of blankets and scissors.

His namesake, a federal electoral division that covered some of Batman's attempted land title, is changed in 2019 to commemorate the Yorta Yorta activist, William Cooper.

Commemorate – to remember together. Naming goes further, perhaps: for worse and better, it keeps history above memory.

But what if there isn't really a person or event to name, so much as a question or a feeling? I think that's why Tom Nicholson makes monuments.

His proposed monument points to the hill where Batman lived, near what is now Southern Cross Station in Narrm, Melbourne. Nicholson's monument connects Batman's dwelling to William Buckley, an escaped English convict who was welcomed by Wathaurong people. Their Country extends from the coast west of Port Phillip, up to Ballarat where the din of the Gold Rush would eventually invade.

Buckley spends thirty years as a Wathaurong man, before walking away from his adopted family in 1835. Once Buckley has glimpsed redcoats on Country and, barely recalling English, has crossed into their colonial complex of Port Phillip, he cannot go back. Buckley is 'the loneliest walker in history…as we go on re-creating him, as he continues walking through the historical landscape at our disposal'.

The material form of Nicholson's artwork is of a pile of red bricks, echoing the chimney that William Buckley – a bricklayer by trade before he was transported – built for John Batman's house. The way that Nicholson has displayed it over the years, the pile could be waiting to be shaped as a chimney, or it may be the ruins of one; or it may simply be a bunch of salvaged material, ready to be repurposed.

Almost like a concertina, the bricks don't have one side. They're a jumble of intersections. They could never fall the same way twice. They could flower into diverging paths. The meaning of this monument isn't really a question of perspective. Like trees whose roots lever up bedrock, Nicholson's monument raises a question of purpose. Who made this?

And then, like a feeling in time, 'the monument disappears'.

Saltmills, County Wexford is in the south-east of Ireland. The salt was milled in the Iron Age and the county is well-known for its neolithic burial sites. Protestant and Anglo-Irish, the Lynn family are more recent arrivals who cling close to the Pale.

In 1853, while Batman's Hill in Melbourne is being optioned for sale to the railways, the Lynn family leaves the safety of the lordship. They land in Victoria and make their way to their new home in Ballarat.

Ballarat is a thick place, a place of overlaps. It's where the descendants of John Curwen-Walker will end up when they leave lutruwita, Tasmania. Typically, the patriarchs of this family are recalled and even publicly noted. But one of them will marry a woman named Bessie Lynn, and from that union descends my mother's father. Ballarat is where he will marry his housekeeper, Nan, and where my mother will grow up. This is a silent lineage, a matriarchal one. So, while I don't feel connected to Bessie, perhaps I should. As a colonial girl, Bessie knows things that others don't.

Bessie Lynn, my great-great-grandmother, has never lived in a tent. One of the littlest of the recently arrived family, she probably doesn't notice the inconvenience as much as her siblings or parents do. While many in Ballarat will continue their lives in tents for years or build huts in the Wathaurong style, the Lynns quickly order the first 'house' in the town. It's important that they have iron and glass to distinguish them from the goldfields: diggers are the reason Bessie's father has brought the family to Ballarat. He has colonial law to sell.

The buyers are a self-organising city of men. From Geelong, Melbourne, Manchuria, California, Holland, Ireland, the

Caribbean, Canada, grabbing at patches of land, yellow rocks underground. Men who are learning to wash, darn and cook for themselves and one another. Men who have families in another country or city, where they send their profits after cashing in nuggets. Guests in a hurry, whose purpose doesn't have time to recognise the system of law that is already around them.

While Bessie's father tries to interpret the rule of the colony, she watches the goldfields from her window. She sees Native Police patrolling the diggings high on horseback, spiffy uniforms with flashing weapons above the mud.

Bessie watches Wathaurong and Djab Wurrung come into town, offering to locate gold or trading their own finds for fancy clothing, transport, food grazed from their homelands. They sell tools and possum rugs to unprepared miners. She imagines the feel of that lush pelt.

Beyond Bessie's window, the Wathaurong continue to meet at the huge swamp. In 1857, she hears percussion and singing carrying into town from a corroboree by the water. Carvings and stonework are dug up by squatters' workers when they sink wells. Livestock are slurping the creeks and mowing through the sweet patches of tubers and grass. Chinese market gardeners sell Bessie's mother greens and fruit instead of more meat and bread. Groups of the diggers' homeless children rove the tent cities. Bessie knows the grid of stores and huts around the main street, but beyond fifty metres she's lost. She pulls her curtains closed.

While the hammer of the black or tin smith, the mallet
of the mason, the trowel of the bricklayer, or the saw
of the carpenter, sent forth no sound

fourteen black-fellows armed
an aboriginal camp
as large as an ordinary-sized circular summer-house,
and rude seats all around.

With the method of harvesting in 1850
the aborigines were numerous about Ballarat.

\

White savages, or as they might by some
be designated glorious, immaculate Britons
wander about in the most
absolutely primitive state of nature.
They are as yet
unfit to be entrusted
with the discharge of the duties; they are not
yet civilised enough, or far enough advanced, for such a privilege.

/

The larger tents were erected over a timber frame and pegged to
the dirt ground 'floor'. Some tents had mud brick fireplaces and
chimneys or alternatively they could have been clad with bark.
Some of the 'tents' were made of bark or were mud huts. Some
were made with primitive timber frames or some were timber

tents in the form of half an open umbrella covered with the skins
of animals.

\

A piece of wood was carved
into the likeness of a human head.
Attached to the head was a continuation
of the block in the form of a shaft.

/

We could not afford
to have an open door;
the arrival of an immigrant ship
having made servants of most kinds temporarily plentiful,
we seldom light a fire to make
a pot of tea or johnnycake.

\

We lived in a sort of
hut built of branches and bark.
Some clad in opossum rugs and others in European attire,
we lived in bark huts, privileged
to cultivate a certain portion of ground.

/

Every morning
before leaving the camp, pick
up every little crumble of bread, bones,
and other scraps –

everything
to learn
from his profession and practice.

\

We lived together and slept in the one tent
cooking for the blacks.

The black troopers were the only mounted police, and indeed
performed all the police duty at the Ballarat Diggings.

/

The owners or occupiers of any house or
building, or of any land where the fence in any way
encroaches on the boundary line of any street, road, common
thoroughfare, or public reserve within the said municipality, will
be required to move such house, building or fence back to the
surveyed line.

\

A new chum who reached Ballarat
took a run at a brushwood fence and landed successfully on the

other side
only to find himself amongst an assortment of blacks
and their dogs all of whom made a great noise
so he jumped quickly back.

/

Ballarat's first house belonged to the late Adam Loftus Lynn
calmly smoking his pipe in his hut
and spitting with perfect serenity on his floor.

The house was shipped from
Richard Todd, of Glasgow, and is identified on the invoice as
'one galvanised iron house'. The house comprised 69 pieces and
three cases. The house was consigned to 'Melbourne, New South
Wales' and this caused considerable delay.

\

When I first
opened the door, and before I came to the
threshold, the man made a movement as if
taking up a position.

The Police Magistrate: And was it in his own house your husband
struck the blow?

Yes.

The Police Magistrate: A very natural thing to do, I should say.

You are discharged.
Go away.

X

Mary Smith, the occupier was sentenced to twelve months for keeping a house frequented by disorderly persons filthier and more frightful than the harpies, who, at the jingle of a coin on the pavement, swarmed in myriads from unseen places, struggling, screaming, shrieking for their prey, like some monstrous and unclean animals.

Among the people who complained of the house were three Chinamen. The 1500 or 1600 Chinese residents of Golden Point live and thrive where an Englishman would starve. The Chinese have more to answer for in this regard than any other class in the community.

X

At Ballarat every man is his own architect. The style of the building is not 'various'. The colour adopted in its decoration externally, renders it no more Moorish or Venetian than Hindoo or Chinese, or another style since style existed.

/

On a piece of flat clear ground
arrive two bullock drays laden with spoil.
The dray is halted and the process of unloading

commences quickly, strewed upon the grass;
and the dray unladen and the drayman paid
his charges, away go both, never,
perchance, to be again seen.

A great portion of the Flat
is already marked out; and it is strange to see parties
haggling over a few inches of boundary wall, when whole acres
are left undisturbed.

In an extensive mia-mia
blackfellows are busy tailoring.
One wing is devoted to the library, of which the public is duly
informed by a painted announcement to that effect over the door.

/

We have advanced to a social state in which domestic comfort
counts for a great deal, and in which the domestic affections have
their full scope.

Several ladies ventured to leave their comfortable homes
in Melbourne and Geelong for the attractive novelties of the
enchantingly distant
'diggings'.

It was deemed proper to place over them a guard
of aboriginal troopers, to protect them and their fragile resting
places from the rude curiosity or molesting propensities of the

bachelor vagrants, the excited homage of the houseless, homeless wifeless diggers.

\

A search was begun and some time later Elizabeth was found safe and well in the Aboriginal camp sucking a possum bone. This woman had been seen in the tent of a man of colour the previous evening.

/

The Chinaman was occupying
Mr Birchett's seat at the table.

\

I care not for grandeur – I care not for wealth;
Nor the glitter of pride's sickly ray;
But a home, with the loved ones all joyous with health,
If it be but a cottage of clay.

No tie upon earth is so strong or so holy
As our home and our household treasures:
Bundles, bags, boxes, tubs, picks, shovels, cradles, axes, hatchets, pannikins, billies, waddies, nullah nullahs, and other weapons.

Wm. WILLIAMS.
Ballarat, Dec. 14th, 1852.

X

The Eureka massacre will be handed down
from father to son.

This birth in blood of a new
nation will not, cannot die. Australia must
pass through the fiery ordeal.

And these poor men will return to this town, and to all your
smaller towns, and villages, and villas, and farms –
idiot faces hardened into a settled leer of mendicancy,
simeous and semi-human.

X

To resist the payment of rents and rates
the white man in Australia is hardly multiplying at all.

Those pallid bodies
on which is stamped the finger of death,
huddled together in such a mass, without the least regard to
order,
might be of great use to many others,
if allowed to remain here.
Australia must have martyrs.

X

From Cabinet members down to
the humblest female servant, nothing of Celtic origin
in the colony's escaped

exclusive use of the whole produce
of the present year's harvest.

X

An error almost fatal
is committed by our authoress
in the pains she takes to paint her
blacks in the very whitest white,
while she is equally careful to disfigure her
whites with the very blackest black.
Few of the fair coloured are warranted, living
or dying, without blemish.

/

At three o'clock,
Mr Lynch mounted a stump on the ground.
When the news of the massacre
reached Melbourne he was one of half a dozen
who turned the tide.

/

The scene of the bloody struggle
between the forces of an oppressive

Government and an oppressed people
who urged even a partially open door:

a case, the parallel of which
has seldom, if ever, been equalled, either for its
atrocity or for the disdain and disrespectful
contempt with which the Government has treated
every communication on the subject
for consideration and reparation.

/

The tent was found; we
approached with caution.
There would be no little danger in
too abrupt a hail. We cooeyed out of reach of
lead. The precaution was no more than prudent.
We were heard; – our business was asked.

Thirteen years before Bessie's family occupied Ballarat, Chief Protector Robinson comes through the area to get a sense of relations between traditional owners and squatters. He is too late for William Buckley.

Robinson meets a party of Wathaurong women digging for tubers with eight-foot-long sticks, and some earthworks near Mount Buninyong: in dry marshes stand conical formations of rock up to seventy feet high, and ploughed earth. He is introduced to a Wathaurong group with syphilis contracted from settler men and is told of a knife attack upon some settlers to the west. He encounters another Wathaurong family from whom a child has been taken by invaders, and who plead Robinson to get the boy back. 'This was a disreputable transaction and the parties ought to be punished for such offences if the blacks are to have the same protection as the whites,' jots Robinson in his journal. Some of his toothless righteousness has returned.

    Although the women continue to dig for the murnong, Robinson believes the yam is already damaged. In fact, he stays at the station of a squatter who cultivates murnong in his veggie patch. Wathaurong people chop wood, hunt eels and do other domestic labour for the more peaceful settlers, in exchange for food. Robinson sees swift parrots and sulphur-crested cockatoos flying over thick fields of kangaroo grass.

    He is much flattered when an ex-Van Diemonian recognises him on a Scottish-owned station. The stockman praises Robinson for the removal of the Palawa from Van Diemen's Land. He says, boasts Robinson, that 'I had increased the value of every person's property in the colony.'

    Robinson asks the stockman if he'd been afraid of Palawa.

Oh no, the stockman replies, forgetting recent history and his interlocutor. 'There was none to be afraid of,' he says, 'they got soldiers and drove them in a corner and took them and put them on a desert island.'

Tunnerminnerwait is not with Robinson on this trip. Rather, some 150 kilometres away to the east of Port Phillip, he is with Maulboyheener and Planobeena, Truganini and Pyterruner. While Robinson files his trauma and sleeps peacefully on the western front, the 'desert island' sojourners are tailing a pair of whalers to the east.

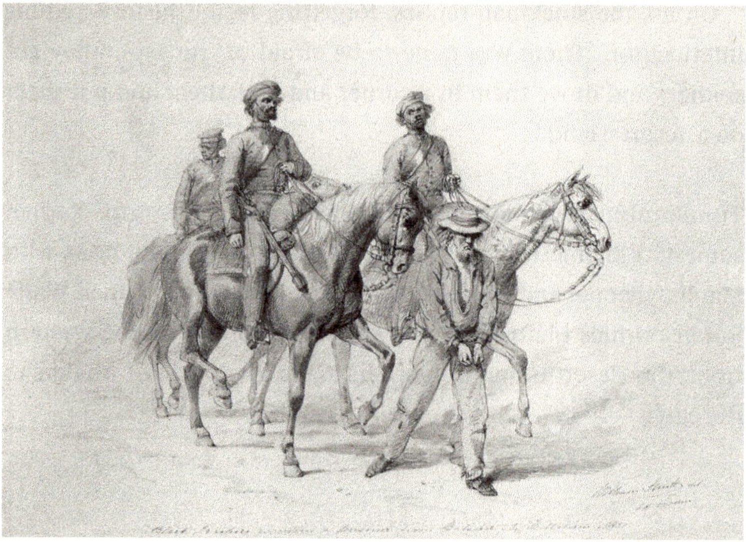

From her window, Bessie sees the wife of James Scobie, a Scottish digger murdered by a publican, approaching the front door.

She hears Mrs Scobie asking for Bessie's father. *There'll be a riot on these conditions,* the disheveled woman is saying to Bessie's mother. *We're wanting an inquest for Jamie, won't Mr Lynn stand?*

Bessie hears, after the door is shut, her mother cursing *redcoats*. She hears, when her father gets home, his cursing *half-human taigs*. It has all *followed us,* he says, *the anger and the blame.*

Not the Orientals, says her mother, *now that's a problem all its own.*

Through her window, Bessie hears women and children running towards Black Hill to a Wathaurong camp. She waits for her mother to call her, that they should follow. She hears a mob of shouting men coming down the street, clanging their pans. A stone comes through the glass.

I don't know what to expect. This is a mourning event but also a recognition of endurance.

By the time I arrive at Lake Wendouree in Ballarat, the surface of the water is stretched with small creases reflecting the rising light. Whenever I'm up at this hour it's as though I've never seen it before: the imperceptible arrival of silhouette, shadow.

There are floodlamps set on a stage beside the lake, a table with a visitor's book, and a deep cone of smoke coming up from the back of the crowd.

I watch the lights reflect off tears and snot silently passing down half-awake faces.

The mood is the colours of the sky – intensely bruised, absorbent grey and jets of summer heat yet to fall. As the morning brightens, people's faces become defined.

The crowd breaks, people look up at the pink cloud and water birds drifting in. Smoke hits the nostrils dry and pungent, transforms tears, and works through clothing and hair. As people move away from the edge of the water, the smoke carries off over the lake.

Three generations of an Indian-Australian family pick their way back to the car park; others stretch out in preparation for their morning jog on the public holiday. Someone's describing their plans for a party in the afternoon.

It is bitter and rousing, solemn and hopeful. I can't think of another local public ritual that invites these blurred emotions, that resists giving its participants fixed phrases or symbols to repeat.

The public holiday is well into gear as I return home from the dawn service.

I left Narrm, Melbourne in 2018, to live on Dja Dja Wurrung land near the goldfields town of Castlemaine. As I curve through the volcanic plains north-east of Ballarat, I'm surrounded by smooth, gold stubs of ancient cores. 'The disruption of here and now.' I pass by Lalgambook, Mount Franklin and recall the Dja Dja Wurrung story of how the upstart mountain and its older neighbour, Tarrengower, created the boulders on the plain.

Bessie Lynn's family knows this plateau even if they didn't know the stories of its making. Does Bessie ever wonder how it came to be?

Australian flags are slung outside houses beside the abandoned Forest Creek diggings. There's the miners' flag over the first 'monster meeting' of diggers, an upswell against licenses and policing that happened a couple of years before the Eureka Rebellion.

That first wave of miners clamoured for their right to dig unimpeded. How did the Eureka Rebellion, like a volcanic eruption, eclipse the already two-decade long series of invasions of Wathaurong and Dja Dja Wurrung?

A second wave of miners, working for companies, would arrive in the next decades to blast the undiggable gold out of the hillsides with water cannon. By the 1870s the goldminers at Forest Creek had turned a valley of creeks and box-ironbark hunting grounds, water wells and quarries into a place the Dja Dja Wurrung now call 'upside down Country'.

My husband is cooking when I get in, he doesn't hear me over the spitting pan. Our dogs, undeterred by the promise of eggs, come barrelling out the door. They shove me so hard that for a few minutes I forget entirely where I've been.

    It's still early morning. We make plans for the day – a walk, a movie – a gorgeously busy noise that fills my consciousness.

It occurs to me that this
is how forgetting feels.
It's as volitional
and lovely as this.

I live in a valley, the anticlines are urgent. They break off and thrust in the creekbed. It filled this winter, orange through the clear. Streams came down from the weir, through the flats, two or three parallel charges. And met in funny corners, confident around the coppiced bulbs of the box gums.

Where is going back to. The creek is upside down.

Near there, the British Queen hotel was established in the 1860s. Its proprietor was Manchurian, as were most of the clientele with a mix of Scottish and Irish diggers. They drank stout over mahjong. The British Queen was flooded and burned down into the Loddon River.

In Sally Potter's *Orlando*, the poet Nicholas Greene says of the Queen: 'Dogs dogs more dogs and far too many rooms.'

Adam Loftus Lynn left one part of the Empire for another, never to return. He thought he'd broken the Queen's spell.

I don't believe that I'll exit the continent; or that the rest of my kind would follow me like rats to new havens. Imagine, though: the re-homing of unsettled White daughters to the globe.

I stood in the queue surrounded by junk and glitter. *New in town?* she turned to face me. So this is what it feels like, I thought. *I'm six generations here* she pointed to the carpet and turned back to face the counter. It feels like.

Remember her name.

I was there buying plastic flowers to put around the corner, outside the Castlemaine lockup. Fresh bunches were too easy to clear away; I'd seen that after Anzac, under the police flagpoles.

I chose flower shapes that resembled native flax and pea. They were rubbery – you could bend the stems and they never snapped.

As I wake up, I recognise her – the woman in the queue. Once she came to clean the many rooms in my house. With her six generations under my landlord's roof. She brought along a seventh, her adult son. My dogs reminded him of the snake under his house. The snake is not a symbol.

In the scree of the creekbank there are smashed plates, one of the fragments with a double rose-coloured border. No one says it's the Queen's.

Maybe she had recognised me, as well, or tried to.

I didn't believe I would purchase stolen land. It would obviously be a 'denial of the original dispossession'.

But when the landlord wanted us to stop revegetating the cleared skeletal soil. My mother asked my dead Nan to look down and find me the place to buy. *Just tell me what else you need* she says. *Nan'll look after you.*

'The future may not be colonised, but it's singed with fires burning so ferociously that they are staining ice caps in Aotearoa,' writes Paola Balla. 'In the wake of climate change caused by colonisation, settlers literally plan how to re-construct, therefore, re-colonise.'

I visit a property for sale that borders Crown land. It's the gold diggings, regrown like a dry jungle. I go to sleep thinking about snake precautions, what with the dogs.

The property overlooks a prison wall. I go up there after dark and look at the floodlights. Medium security, men. My friend teaches there. *Best students I ever had* she says after her first week. There are often workplace incidents she can't tell me about. *I know some things* she'll say or *Something happened. But I'm not allowed to tell.* I change the subject so she isn't tempted, though I'm not sure who I'm protecting.

The creek slows down and hangs onto water. No one says it's going to return.

Writing *Chatelaine* I thought about the house as a pretense, a stage. I moved every two years, I took more rooms. When I left I was told to return the property to its original condition.

My mother and I have been talking about Nan's secrets and lies. Nan's parents went to Aotearoa and left she and her sister behind in Victoria with her German grandfather. Her parents had more children, including one her father had with a Māori woman. When Nan grew up she worked as a housekeeper then married her employer – my mother's father – in Ballarat. Despite all the houses, she didn't have many rooms. There was nowhere to go back to.

I went back to the landlord's place to retrieve our tat. He was already there, cutting down one of two gums left on the hillside and pissing on the sandstone reef where I'd put water-retaining clumps of tussock and sedge.

Perhaps I think I've broken the spell. The land I have bought is not a stage, it cannot be emptied of dignity as though it were furniture.

The insurer declares the fire risk extremely high. There are real flax and pea but timber harvesting has made the bush thick. I know that we might run out of time to future-proof the spongy soil. I consider asking my dead nan for help.

When the fire comes and what's left is my title, unextinguished.

Trespass

New England, New South Wales
(1850–1900)

Mary Sweeney – Thomas Cassidy   Arthur Hanratty – Eleanor Ryan
            | |
——————————————————   Mary Ann – –
| | | | | | | | |
Patrick John Margaret Rebecca Terence &c   –
                            | |
                            –   –
                            | |
                        My father's father – My father's mother
                            |
                        My father

In *Blakwork,* Gomeroi writer Alison Whittaker reflects on the tiresome labour of quelling settler anxiety:

> That dawdling off-trend meme,
> white guilt.   To survive among it, well,
>
>   it's naff to say, but compul –
>   – sory to do. Indentured blakwork,
>   something like:
>
>   nine to five, forgiv –
>   – ing you.

Guilt's not my foible; it's wanting to know.

I'm the wannabe clubber at the top of the queue, insisting my ID's legit. *It's accepted everywhere else*, I want to say. *Look*, I point out what it says beneath my photo: *Writer.*

Should I go home? I'm not even sure the bouncer has seen me. And no, he's not big and black. She looks a bit like me. Sipping a Red Bull. Saying, *step back*. Righteously, *make way*.

Everyone's a member but I'm insisting on admission to the balcony – the place with a view.

And this is what I tell myself I'm going to do there: I can look, but not take. I can watch, but not photograph. I can make notes, but not conclusions.

Who am I kidding? It's a hustle. To get there I'm going to push past others, nudge them with my totebag of Moleskine notebooks, climb up the stairs which means forcing people to stand up and move aside, and when I get up there I'm going to start asking for a smoke, or getting someone to hold my drink, or block someone

133

else's line of sight. Do I know what's gone down in this place?

Do I still want to go in? Am I going to make good use of that view? Can I even see that much?

And when do questions become another tedious White demand?

The art teacher pulled down the blinds and turned on the TV.

The deep blue, dusk lighting; the red stones on the studio floor. The brown boy laughing in the surf, the brown girl crying. I wondered why the children had a White mother.

Not long after that class, the evening news showed masses of people walking across the Sydney Harbour Bridge. *SORRY* said their banners and pickets. But still I wondered why the strong Aboriginal woman in the film bothered caring for the frail White lady.

/

The drama teacher took the class to see Louis Nowra's *The Golden Age*. I felt like a child behind a door, hearing the adults talking but barely making out what was being said.

My brother had moved out of home, so my parents took me on a roadtrip around Tasmania. In the servos, the newspapers were running stories about fabrication. I got my first period at a manor house at Richmond. Back home I educated myself about the Black War. I tried writing a play about two sisters and their black servant for the drama teacher. I couldn't tell that story yet.

/

The history teacher gave a unit on the Myall Creek massacre.

In the winter holidays, my uncle drove us into New England. It might have been the last camping trip we all made together, since my cousins and my brother were young adults, and I was well into the frowning funk of adolescence. It was foggy and wet, we climbed what seemed to be vertical roads above cattle pastures.

There was some talk between my father and my aunt about their family's history in the region. We ended up before a sign on a cliff edge. The fog was lifting away and I could see that my feet were on that ground.

Cognitive dissonance allowed my father to compartmentalise a number of parallel realities so that they might exist without harming him.

The thing is, when he was lying about his whereabouts and expenses, he didn't just believe he was in control of the boundaries between those realities; he *was*. The rest of us were successfully coerced by his control of information about the past and present.

It's not so different to the effects of nationalism, a story started by late nineteenth-century settler Australians and believed by us, their descendants to this day. Not so different to the way that governments and institutions can executively control that national story through communications of denial. Mark McKenna also uses the image of rooms when he refers to a culture of forgetting colonial encounter: 'If I remain unaware of this past, I feel as if I am living in one room of a house, in which all the other rooms remain closed.' W.E.H. Stanner identified this as the 'Great Australian Silence' of 'disremembering'.

To use a different metaphor, my father's coercion was not so different to the way that story cuts off the limbs that reach out into different directions from the past, trims the past down, shears that trunk that connects it to the present, leaves a stub of truth.

I am borrowing this tree from Gladys and Jill Milroy, Palyku women. They talk about how settlers 'create separate stories' from big, continuous ones; how we sever past from present and future. They call it 'dis(re)membering'.

We select parts of the story about ourselves and cut the links between them. That's when psychologists say we become 'fused'. These stumpy stories limit our agility. Whose perspective can we no longer imagine? What knowledge can we no longer access?

Which names can we not say?

By its nature, a habit of dis(re)membering obscures its own beginnings. Could my father have said when he began to label and separate mutually incompatible scenarios and people? This habit, this culture, creates denial, or silence. Without a language we can't corroborate a relationship or an event as having happened. Without a way to collect memory we miss out on listening. When we stop listening we forget.

> ...the inhabitants some time ago made a collection
> for the making and baking of a kiln of bricks,
> and there it stands, like the Tower of Babel,
> a mass of bricks, as a momento [sic]
> (not of the confusion of tongues),
> but a diversity of creeds, some wishing them to be used
> for a Presbyterian, others Episcopalian, and some for a Catholic place
> of worship;
> so between conflicting opinions,
> we are without any place.

Mary Ann's parents pick the pockets of County Monaghan.

In the following century, the partition of Ireland will make Monaghan one of the volatile Republican border counties. Until then the Gaelic peasantry are squeezed by tithes, enclosure, labour, famine and threat until they either get themselves transported, or flee.

Her parents fall into the latter category, are caught and shipped to Sydney; but somehow, on getting free they find one another again. They marry in 1835.

From first sentencing until death, her mother racks up a spree of robbery, arson, obscene language and drunkenness. Drowns in a puddle.

Her father diversifies, stealing cattle and horses and doing time in the best places – Norfolk Island, Port Arthur, Darlinghurst Gaol, Cockatoo Island.

In the midst of it, in spite of it, she grows: baby Mary Ann is born in 1837 at Clarence Town, a logging hamlet on the Williams River in the Hunter Region of New South Wales.

The last time Mary Ann Ryan is recorded living with her parents is 1841, aged four. Later in life, the only thing she can remember from that time is the kiln and the pile of bricks at Clarence Town. After that her mother and father are each gaoled, their waif becomes a ward of the state who lives only in the present.

Mary Ann is my father's great-great-grandmother, but this is the first I've heard of her. I find her on the internet. She is not recalled as a matriarch or even as a good story. I forgive her descendants for forgetting her, and myself for not asking until now. She's White trash – and she's something else, something bothersome to colonial society and the sort of psyche it creates, something the Irish journalist Fintan O'Toole might call an unknown known.

As a ward, she may be boarded out to the care of a family or locked up at the Female Orphan School. If she is in an institution, then Mary Ann will be accommodated with girls like mirrors of herself, and First Nations girls from the Hunter Valley who've fallen prey to police or missionary surveillance.

The Commissioner of Lands in the Hunter is Mary Ann's state guardian. When she turns fifteen, he approves her marriage to a middle-aged, English ex-con. How can I know whether this is sanctioned trafficking or true love? How often does the Commissioner approve or even initiate such matches? Mary Ann Ryan appears mature for her age, but she is also a deeply traumatised teenager. For whatever reason she has taken her mother's name.

Mary Ann and her husband move to Armidale in New England,

that lip of tableland beneath the border of New South Wales and Queensland. They quickly start a family. Her husband dies when Mary Ann is twenty-two. She marries again at Armidale. She has fourteen children by the two men, but her offspring either abandon her or are also poverty stricken; she dies in an asylum for poor women.

I don't feel much for Mary Ann or her hopeless parents, except amazement that they cling onto life at all. And, they cling onto me somehow – the story of their settlement is as real and contingent as anybody else's. It may or may not be part of me, but maybe it tells me something useful.

In a settler family culture, Mary Ann is too far away in time to be remembered, and for the living she is a sad story. We feel somehow responsible for her sadness, and instinctively pull away from its suction.

Where does Mary Ann Ryan belong? It isn't the pre-Famine Ireland of her parents; she can't have known it and can never get back to her kin. Is it Clarence Town, her birthplace: the river port of convict labour, Gringai raids and timber-getters?

Perhaps it is New England, the Anaiwan Country of Armidale where she makes her own family, and which comes closest to a chosen home.

Or maybe she only ever feels at home within the institutional walls where she grows up and dies.

In *Amnesia Road*, Luke Stegemann anticipates our recoil from Mary Ann's story. 'The past risks being conceived as a wasteland of mistakes, ill habits and unproductive relationships; a fruitless and toxic place from which, if any lesson might be gleaned, it is only this: *do not go back.*'

Back there, behind a 'culture of deliberate unknowing', is a pregnant teenager from an industrial school.

In 1852, as a fifteen-year-old wife, Mary Ann Ryan arrives to live on stolen Anaiwan land in Armidale.

Anaiwan historian Callum Clayton-Dixon collates all the references to 'native dogs' in the diary of John Connal, an Armidale grazier. When Mary Ann begins her married life nearby, Connal has already recorded twenty-six dingo kills in six months. Mostly he uses his kangaroo dogs to hunt the dingoes. He intends to eliminate and to remember it.

While Connal does his best to inscribe erasure in blood and ink, he doesn't fully succeed. As for Mary Ann, she goes to sleep in the archive.

I've no diary from Mary Ann. That is, she does not remember herself.

But at the place where they both dwell, the ground tells other stories.

I have no diary from my father.

His denial was not because of Anaiwan and Ngarabal lands. Those Countries take in his forebears and hold them for generations.

Do our kin love that ground? Perhaps. But by the time his father leaves New England in the Depression, it has been fully fabricated into 'Celtic Country'. A silence has descended, which draws like fog as the land is cleared.

'Everyone talks proudly of their family trees but not everyone talks about the trees in their families,' say Gladys and Jill Milroy.

This not talking: does it start with the quieting of the original names of the Country? Or is it the silencing of the bad times that Irish immigrants fled, the self-preserving forward motion; the shame of men or the resilience of women? Does its origin matter anymore?

So I decide to listen for the trees – and the other plants, animals, fungi connected to them, and the other people they have nourished – who stand by much longer memories.

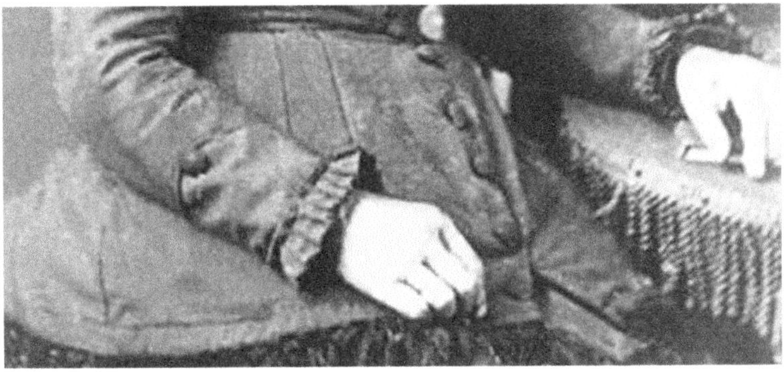

Eating aerial views of the dividing range, holding off the sight of rubbish collecting down below in the crevices of roots

sounds like you're

talking quietly to yourself

happening to somebody else.

I was about six when I dreamed up an imaginary friend named Mary. Mary was older, somewhat prim. She would come and go of her own whim and seemed to know something I didn't. Mary was sage. I told myself *Mary stories* which I guess were a sort of chronicle. I'm not sure I ever wrote them down. And then Mary faded back forever into my dreams.

This is also a Mary story.

This Mary is an assemblage from local archives and newspapers, Anaiwan and Ngarabal oral histories and settler stories. Like young Mary Ann Ryan, like my imaginary friend, this Mary Cassidy becomes unknown. So we lose the story of flooded creeks, scarred trees, bark walls and resilient communities that enable her long widowhood in northern New South Wales.

We all know the story of Thomas Cassidy. Once upon, Thomas is transported to Sydney for murdering a horse.

Irish landowners, many of them of English origin, were largely absentees. They, or their agents, presided over a scene of wretched and hopeless poverty, in which their main object was to extract the maximum in rent… 'for once, the peasantry had gained the whip hand. Murder, arson, the maiming of cattle and boycotting were amongst the weapons they used in their desperate, and largely successful, efforts to prevent the landlords.'

Were he living in a different part of Ireland, Thomas might be amongst those scaring the Lynn family out of the country. Some of Thomas's fellow resistors go to the barricade of the Eureka Rebellion in Ballarat. But he stays in Sydney, where he meets Mary Sweeney, a free woman and a housemaid, and a fellow Gael from the Shannon River estuaries.

On her departure from Ireland to employment, Mary is certified of 'very good' character. 'Bodily health and probable usefulness' are also good. She is 'a strongly built woman with fairer and wavy hair'.

Having served his time, naturally Thomas becomes a police constable at Parramatta. It's another case of unknown knowns for a colonial culture, that ex-convicts and former rebels will don a badge and begin to enforce the law. Thomas and Mary live a couple of decades in western Sydney and have many children. I don't know if life is happy or not, but they stay together, employed, and their kids stay educated and close.

After Thomas, Mary Cassidy does not die of grief. She carries on with her children for about a decade at the fringes of Sydney. That place is now called Pemulwuy. And then, about 1870 she moves the Cassidy family northward to New England. She begins her next life.

All persons found TRESPASSING on my property (Prospect Valley, Beardy Plain) without my consent, after this date, will be prosecuted without respect to party or persons.
MARY CASSIDY
Glen Innes, 15th November, 1884

But no one seems to know this chapter. Mary's property no longer exists. There's no sign, no photo, no sketch. There's not even a brick. I go by the maps of her titles and fill in a space between the boundary lines.

Fences aren't up; stock roam, are stolen, rebranded. Big stations in the district depend on Ngarabal or Anaiwan labour to ride the boundaries. You could say, Mary Cassidy's property has never existed.

From the street, I find a door ajar. It's mid-morning and already the sun is penetrating the back of my neck. The tops of my shoulders feel like tiny bitumen car parks. I can hear splashes and quiet voices on the other side of the door. Leaning into it, I make my way through some sort of abandoned briefing room – bags, a whiteboard, drink bottles – and out the other side, into the pool complex.

The public pool: a great denominator. In the social lane, a few people with Down's syndrome do laps as middle-aged parents watch from the benches. In the fast lane, a couple of wiry, tanned septuagenarians finish their morning sprint and haul out. Waiting for them is an elderly woman with fat-draped thighs. When Charles Perkins took the Freedom Ride to Moree, it was the public pool that he targeted as the site of equality.

'How'd you get in here?' He's resting his arms on the edge, wiping water off his forehead as I try to open the gate.

I'm holding my shoes in the same hand I'm using to lift the gate lock. 'Sorry?'

'Who let you in? Only squad's allowed in before ten.'

I look back at the big digital clock over the kiosk building. 9.58. 'That door,' I point towards the squad room, 'was open. And I paid the girls at the counter over there.'

'Not when the roller door is shut. You have to wait outside until it's open. In future. Please.'

It's true, there's a very closed roller door behind the kiosk counter. I feel the prickly lawn under my bare feet. I imagine all the folks of Armidale that must be standing in a queue on the other side of the door, in that sun.

I give up fumbling with the pool gate and sit down on the grass. It seems the fair thing to do. Three minutes later, I hear the roller door furling up. From under a sweeping jacaranda, I look through it to the oblong of stark light reflecting off the pavement outside. And in they come, my fellow paddlers. A rogue sandy-coloured dog pushes through and, for a couple of seconds, it's one of us inside the oasis – before the pool man, wet-haired and now dressed in his red and yellow staff polo, ducks in front of the dog and shoos it back into the street.

'New England was a two-class society.'

'Was?' I ask.

The archivist smiles. 'Yeah, it's still there, you just have to scratch the surface a bit.' He's a rumpled, softly spoken man. The way he sees his job, he explains, is 'to provide ammunition to both sides'.

I envision a cattle queen with a popped collar, hiding behind a topiary hedge while most of Armidale's population lays claim to her cellar of Grange.

I tell him that George Augustus Robinson called the Western District of Victoria *two-faced*. The archivist is quick to laugh but I wonder if something accumulates in the bones from spending years around these archives.

He shows me how maps reveal the way people moved through the New England 'frontier'. 'That's how you can see the communications,' he says, unrolling a map the size of a picnic blanket.

'You mean the post?'

'No,' he chuckles. 'Communications means...getting around.'

Before they renamed New England settlements, squatters annexed Anaiwan, Ngarabal and Gamilaroi lands in the 1820s and 1830s. Like in the Western District, these huge runs metastasised villages, parishes and smaller farms, which were generally named after these early pastoral runs, even once the squatters had gone. In the same way, common roads would follow the early pastoralists' sheep tracks. These long paddocks could span hundreds of kilometres, following waterways over the traditional trade routes, or connecting vast chunks of stolen land.

'There were a lot of drownings,' the archivist says out of the blue. Well before municipal councils were formed, he explains, the overland tracks crossed the rivers. In the 1870s high roads were constructed to hug elevated hillsides, forming safer but less efficient routes. 'It was better when there were the old tracks 'cos you could just go straight,' the archivist says, as though reminiscing about a past life.

Terence and Jo Cassidy are being sent ahead. Or Jo is going ahead and Terry is following because he's twelve years old and pretty annoying. Twelve years in western Sydney yet he's learned nothing useful. Jo can ride rodeo, build a sideboard and punch the lights out of his friends. Jo's new wife is waiting at Wellingrove. He is twenty-eight, but still.

On their first night out, Jo teaches Terry to boil a billy. That'll be the younger's job for the next month, if they make it to Glen Innes by December; if they don't, it'll be his job for the next two months or more. It took the Morans nearly twelve weeks to get to Armidale because of the floods.

Mary had a big prayer session on the sitting room floor the night before the boys set out. The girls came home from school in Sydney to help prepare the food and packing for Jo and Terry. They went around lighting all the lamps until the room looked grand but smelled like a pig's belly.

Terry is wondering if he and Jo will keep up their evening prayers while they are away from their mother. Ma Mary, Saint Mary, St Ma, Mrs Mary. Twelve-year-old boys don't think of their mums often, but their dad is very dead, so she is that much more in their lives. She has big arms. Maybe that's where Jo gets his boxing muscles.

Mary doesn't use hers that way anyhow. She says that their da was *a fighter* but not in that way, either. It was because he'd tried to make a point of justice. And he won, she adds. None of the kids raises the question of how their da won since he was transported. To put it more finely, he and his brother pushed their landlord's horse off a cliff at Boho. So. The punishment is beside the point,

Maggie is saying. What's a landlord? asks Terry. Yer nob, says Jo. They made Da pay to live on his own land, says Paddy.

Now Jo and Terry are sitting at the limits of Dharug Country in the dark. Next day they'll cross the Hawkesbury and push into the places Terry has never seen. Two fellows drowned on the swollen river a few months back. The flood wrack is visible along the road below, approaching the punt jetty. When they stopped for the evening, Jo pointed further downriver where drifts of sand had washed into the waterside paddocks. Every chain of land on the banks is farmed. Last light falls onto the sandstone walls on the other side of the water, like fortifications against all that drift. Terry imagines what he'd look like to someone standing on those rock walls: a pebble about to tumble away. They can hear their small mob of cattle crunching around the campsite, and the low river tide like sleeping breath.

In the centre of Armidale, New England, a grove. Black peppermint, gently shading granite. A seasoned trunk stands, lettered

c
o
u
n
t
r
y
t
h
a
t
b
u
i
l
t
m
y
h
e
a
r
t

Judith Wright's poem 'Train Journey' wakes up on an overnight rail trip and sees the New England ranges and plains under moonlight. All her poems about this region pay tribute to its anti-pastoral character. The best ones love it because of its human difficulties.

At the centre of the grove is a boulder with a plaque attached. It says the rock was taken from the Wright family's Wallamumbi station. It says

South of my days' circle, part of my blood's country,
rises that tableland, high delicate outline
of bony slopes wincing under the winter,
low trees blue-leaved and olive, outcropping granite –
clean, lean, hungry country.

The plaque is missing the rest of the poem, the part where those famous lines begin to resemble an old settler's yarn

a story old Dan can spin into a blanket against the winter.
Seventy years of stories he clutches round his bones.
Seventy years are hived in him like old honey.

An old settler who remembers a place on the edge of invasive settlement, a place soon to be forgotten as his generation ages.

Wake, old man. This is winter, and the yarns are over.
No-one is listening.

The lettered trunk and the plaque are polite offerings. Not the place for Wright's more questioning lines towards her squatter forebears ('Nigger's Leap, New England') and Armidale ('Country Town').

In the ladies lounge of a renovated pub, I meet Caroline. Volunteer genealogist, librarian, amateur historian, database maker of New England Aboriginal history. At home, she says, her son sits up at her computer, pretending to type: *'My name's Caroline and I research blackfellas.'*

'I see my role as passing information around,' she suggests. A settler, she gets hold of public records that the public can't find. Speaking with her reminds me that my access to research training, internet, institutional collections is so easy; and that my history is simply hidden and lost, not destroyed or stolen. It's not so easy for everybody with questions about their family.

Caroline shows me chapters on colonisation that she's written for a couple of local history books. A frown. 'I could have put more in,' she sighs, 'I could have really pushed it.' She points at a paragraph about an alleged massacre site. The property owner denied Caroline access – and denied the event. Is this what the archivist meant by 'both sides'?

That didn't happen here

On January 26, Caroline joined the Survival Day march through town. Meanwhile, down the street, 'About fifty people turned up to the awards for White people,' she shrugs.

Caroline goes to confession when it's necessary. 'You own your actions,' she explains. She doesn't read fiction. 'Fantasy and all that... You can't back it up!'

Mary makes it through the big drought, reducing her cattle stock as the lagoon line drops and then evaporates into a deep, black bog. Rebecca damps down the floor and re-does the exploded paper on the walls. Terry, returning home via the back road, says there's a burial found at Red Range. The cleared earth must have been eroding away. The remains are unearthed on the huge run that neighbours the Cassidys at Beardy Plain.

Mary watches as the bones are arranged into a small pile at the foot of the range. As a girl she'd a fantasy about getting a bit of Saint Brigid's bone. Now that craving feels a long way away. It is a man's skeleton, she reads later, and it has been sent away to Sydney. She makes a prayer for that soul.

The land that holds them is ear-poppingly high, of plains run with deep, mossy creeks and ringed with gently domed hills. Granite tors tumble out of the earth. Snow gums and gold banksia make groves where the constant wind hangs back, but these small parks have long been cleared to open paddocks dotted with shoulder-high stumps. A few months later she will see the plains flood, the waters cutting off her land from town. When it subsides, she will watch a dense undergrowth appearing amongst the tracts of ringbarked gums.

We imagine counterfactual histories all the time.

What if I'd grown up with half-sisters?

What if Mary Cassidy hears nothing of the 'colonial apocalypse' that preceded her in New England?

What if all the Ngoorabal and Anaiwan peoples die quietly on reserves and missions?

What if her whole community is European?

What if she builds a life in New England solely through settler-created bushcraft and resources?

What if she doesn't notice that the loud plovers have stopped nesting on the grass by the marshes, and that red foxes are becoming a regular sight across the plains at dawn?

Settler dreams are made of counterfacts. Without stopping to properly hear truths about our past, we have constructed fantasies. What if we tried forgetting some of these? What memories, left behind for us to find, might be recovered? And what good might the settler imagination do with this knowledge, other than legitimise itself?

In August she takes the muslin bag of honeycomb as it passes around the circle. Pale thin liquid drains through the bag into the crevices of her chapped palms. She does as the others have: careful not to lose any of the honey, she lets it run into her tea mug. She watches it curving through the milk. Half of Mary's china beakers got chipped on the journey up. Most of the ones they are holding have stumps where there'd been handles.

Behind the men's heads, where the cleared hillside runs into an open grove of pink-blossomed ironbarks, she sees the ladder of wedges that the axeman cut up one trunk towards the hive. She's made the tea the Sweeney way, left too long until the billy cools and the tannins begin to turn bitter. She looks around at the Ngarabal men wrapping up their axes, then her sons, and muses on whether this is the first trade or the final one.

Some of the Ngarabal men return when Mary begins to prepare slabs for the hut. Terry, now fifteen, works out the price and a few of the men come with bark sheets balanced on horsebacks. Terry rings the blackbutts on the ridge and the slabs they produce are half a foot thick and six foot tall.

Mary notices he's felled the one that was crosshatched like a leadlight pane. Terry turns its scarred face to the earth when the bark sellers come. Her chilled cheeks get hot with annoyance and fear; who'd forget such a tree? What man who spends his skills with an axe wouldn't notice his craftwork missing? Next time the Ngarabal travel over the ridge they'll see it is gone. How do they do their magic here? Where she grew up they'd send the *púca* against you for something like that.

She lashes the bark sheets over the central poles and makes a roof. She hangs the rest of the bark over the empty windows. Her eldest daughters Eliza and Rebecca lime the walls and posts and small Maggie papers the insides of the hut. Even under autumn cloudbanks, the interior glows dimly.

One of the bark seller's wives has given Mary a tea-tree broom for the floor; the hardswept dirt muffles their feet moving from hearth to bed to basin. Jo sinks a dunny pit down the back, but they opt for the pot the first few, late winter nights.

I don't feel troubled by the Hurry Boys on the highway. If I get off the main road to where I want to be, along the waterways, then I can trundle at my own speed. I trust my car. Until I find the turn-off, I pump the pedal and dare anyone to overtake me. One does and it's like a reward for my passivity as I let him sweep into the distance up a crest towards an oncoming freight truck that only I can see.

When I first toured these backroads, I developed a paranoia that white utes were surveilling me. Every time I slowed down or pulled over to look at the drained lagoons or a fine old box gum, a white ute would round the bend and either park a few hundred metres away or pass by again ten minutes later. I couldn't tell whether it was the same vehicle or several. Were they protecting something invisible, or just overseeing the calves chewing along the verge? These were public roads, after all; used mainly by graziers, sure, but public. Anyway, I let it go; my annoyance seems to originate in some proprietorial feeling of my own, which isn't only baseless but doesn't make any sense as a response to someone else's boundary-keeping.

I choose an exit onto a poorly sealed byroad. It's too beautiful, this free access alongside a broad creek lined with sedge, gnarly blackwoods and purple limonium. The water's surface is still and opaque. Mizzling.

There are pied cormorants on boughs and sunken posts, and further down a wheeling flock of black ducks. The palette is mainly just two green tones (bright olive sedge and a lime note in the panic grass), plus some rustiness on the reeds and algal blooms, the inky water, ducks and cows, and then grey clouds. That's blue, yellow, red, black and white.

After sketching I walk back to my car, past some picnic shelters. Native bread busts out of the earth nearby, I realise it's late autumn again. I WANT TO FUCK YOUR SON, it says in Texta on the shelters. FIFTY DOLLARS. Then a vehicle description and a full street address. When I'll tell my friend about this later, she'll say the message is an act of retribution. Her little boy will hop through their front door waving a tiny Australian flag, his freebie from Bunnings.

I pull back onto the highway ready to piss someone off, but the road has emptied. A trace of useless guilt, crystallised into anger, has entered my nerves. I drive waiting.

'We pushed,' Eric Rolls writes in *A Million Wild Acres*, 'along Monument Road, then only a grader track... No one knows how the road got its name.'

At each town going west from Glen Innes – Inverell, Bingara – folks are walking sleepy-eyed from dawn services. Shopfronts roll up and families drive into the main street for breakfast.

Judith Wright knew that 'The earth along the Namoi, the Gwydir and beyond drank much blood' from her family history, *The Cry for the Dead*. And knew, in her poem 'Nigger's Leap, New England' that denial had become forgetting:

Did we not know their blood channelled our rivers,
and the black dust our crops ate was their dust?

There's no tree inscribed with those words, here.
    The Myall Creek Massacre Memorial traces a winding, red-earthed path to an outlook above the creek.
    There are places to sit, walk off the track, leave offerings. No one else arrives while I'm at the memorial, but there are signs of them all around – flowers and stones on the boulders.

On an island in a lake in County Fermanagh, rural Northern Ireland, a two-faced stone figure squats in a pagan graveyard. Thomas Cassidy's ancestors embedded themselves like a boulder beside the lake, maybe two thousand years ago. For maybe one thousand years people have placed coins in the figure's indentations. It faces forwards and backwards; but its origins and its purpose are unknown.

Without a story in which it can live, it is meaningless. Those who knew were encouraged not to know; not to go back. I hear shots on the plains below, a gas gun to ward off cockatoos.

Her Terry has been gone since the chill left the morning air. Mary prays the liturgy while cooking, herding and washing. In the evening Rebecca comes up from the house she and her husband have built over the crest. Mary asks her to ride around and do the asking.

Rebecca starts at all the station camps in the valley. Some of the Ngarabal women are off shepherding. At Shannon Vale, their men are frying mutton over the dinner fire. *Meet Sophia*, Bill laughs, shaking the enamel plate at her. He is the head-man here most seasons. *Sit down?* The smell of hot grease is comforting but Rebecca is too distracted to join them. They haven't seen Terry near the women, and she returns to Mary with nothing.

It's Hamid who will bring the rumour. Weeks later, as though he's recalling an item packaged up in the drawers of his sales cart, he will casually mention that Terry bought a cheap lace collar from him by the road at Bald Nob.

Mary drives herself at first light. There are always unknown men dying out in the cold, people see them lugging their bedrolls by the road and keep driving. Terry isn't unknown and he has been reported, she tries to comfort herself. As the track gently rides the plain, it ascends slightly and she finds herself driving the cart towards clearings of mist between dimpled scribbly gums. Mary pulls up. *I've come to look for Terence*, she says to the trees. By the track's edge, a floor of moss and granite chunks run away into the forest. At the crumble of a stone under hoof, roos appear and then flee into trunks. She isn't going to find him here.

When Mary gets back home the trough has filled with rain. Her mare won't drink, though, and whinnies. She looks back to see a white draught horse peering at them through knotted hair. It has a mess of different brands on one shoulder.

So someone is helping their stock to her grass now.

Maggie isn't in the house. Mary guesses where she's gone. When the youngest girl comes home for school holidays, she and brother Paddy collect dog scalps for bounty. The two of them drag a dead calf to the edge of the property, tap it with rat poison. They leave it one night, maybe two, and then come back for the scalps. The dead pups they find are fluffy and mostly tan, sometimes black with a pale blaze. They are mixed with hunting dogs, these days; the early folks shot out most of the purebreds. Paddy and Maggie split the bounty. They don't usually bother burning the remains; if eagles and crows eat the poisoned guts, they argued, more's the better for the new calves. Sometimes, though, Mary insists that they clean up in case a bagman goes foraging for a feed.

Mary shoohs the white horse and it blinks. She isn't feeling kindly about foragers today, or anything else that wants to let itself into her land. When Paddy and Maggie return from their work a few hours later, Mary makes sure they've left the poisoned carcasses out this time.

What was that song again, 'The Ranger'?

Last year Terry had come home singing it early one morning. Mary heard his horse over the soggy ground before she saw him coming up the valley through long strands of fog. He sat around outside in the first light, drunk as the Devil and belting out that song. His back was still wet from where he'd kipped halfway home. Steam plumed off a pile of dung as the horse stood exhausted, sucking dew off the grass.

These dances, they go on around the creeks beyond the mines. She doesn't ask her sons about girls. There are more Chinese up there than Whites, so.

The Chinese miners pass through Glen Innes, mostly on foot with just a small bundle each. They sometimes rest in town overnight before trudging onwards to the tin fields. Buying new boots for Maggie at Kwong Sing, she listens to their language over the counter and tries to match a sound with the object being purchased.

The bark sellers have their reserve over that way, too. No one wants bark sheets quite as much any longer, when they can get hold of iron. She wonders what the men are selling or exchanging now. Maybe they are digging for tin and gold, too.

Yes, she thinks about grandchildren who don't look much like her. She thinks about that and even prays. For grace to help her love them. Not to ask, not to say.

What was that song again? About a wandering drover and his motley mates. As he passes down the road, it goes, children cry out a warning to their mother.

While I am leaning over the arteries of New England in the archive, its pounding inland heat is punctured by a storm. Two weather systems over the Dividing Range: within an afternoon, a settler's overland journey might be literally toppled from its course.

Local passengers bound for Sydney, trudging beside the bullock dray, might have to camp until the storm passes. I think of the swagmen sometimes reported in the local papers, dead from exposure or campfire, faces eaten by dogs under their bark gunyahs. I think of Beardy Plain up on the northern tablelands, where the swamp below Mary Cassidy's property will be gathering volume. Spoonbills stalk and nest around the weeds. The perennial wind runs through the seeding grassheads. And higher, at Bald Nob, rain sheeting over granite. And over the bark roofs of all the selectors' houses, over the greasy sheep in their bough yards. The yards made by stockmen who are sheltering inside a huge stable. One slate tile, blue with wet, falling over an eave and into a puddle. The wet government blankets around the miners' shoulders at Oban. Suckers sprouting from the ringbarked hillside. An old axe quarry slick of dust. Bounty hunters pulling the wallaby scalps in from their drying place, unpegging them slippery from bark boards. Trying to get a pipe lit while drops come through bark sheets. Keeping the dogs close. The crown of a skull appearing at the bottom of a worksite in town. A Chinese market garden stretching its green leaves into the moist air. Turtle hatchlings grasp at worms. A trader, pushing his *kufi* down closer, hopping inside his wagon and shutting the canvas tight.

As I cross the road to the car, my sandals collect rainwater. I take off the shoes and dip my feet in the rushing gutter.

In 1877, Tommy McPherson, or 'Yarrow Creek Tommy' or 'Black Tommy', murders another First Nations man and hits the road. (Where is Tommy's voice? I am not able to find it or, not meant to.)

He has been captured before – last time, the police had to stop in at Beardy Plain and borrow a cart to transport Tommy to the lock-up. (He fought back.)

Tommy does time on a road-gang. (Making those high roads for the new council, no more shortcuts.) He is known as a wrestler and for his yarning. He isn't yet a killer.

He drinks at the Mount Pleasant Hotel, where he and publican Mrs Quinlan have worked out a way to abide the 1867 Supply of Liquor Act. (Since she isn't permitted to sell or serve him booze, Tommy will leave some money on the bar then go around behind it to pour himself.)

A reward is issued for his apprehension. He hides out around the Mann River area outside of Glen Innes for two years armed with a tomahawk and gun. (Mary Cassidy's youngest, Maggie, has just made her final trip home from boarding school. To do so, she's had to catch the train from Sydney to Morpeth, then follow one of the bullock drays that carts passengers and mail up to the tablelands of northern New South Wales. It's a month of traipsing and riding, nevermind stick-ups.)

Tommy gets food from Mary's neighbour Fletcher, at Bald Nob. (Anaiwan and Ngarabal groups on regular camping routes might drop in to a known friendly place for food. Some might take a bit of fruit from orchards. Swagmen are also expected to come by of an evening to doss down or beg something to eat outside. There is one selector south of Glen Innes who even stocks a pantry of items in a shelter at his gate.) Tommy also likes kangaroo dogs, and borrows them from Fletcher's when he goes up the range to hide. In 1879, he is shot dead at his camp at Bald Nob.

Then, in the late 1880s, another Tommy appears. Tommy Ryan, 'the notorious aboriginal desperado', plays a long game of cat and mouse near Grafton, over the Dividing Range from Glen Innes. (Just after Mary Cassidy dies the ruthless Governor brothers will begin their spree.)

The Cassidys read and gossip about these rovers just as they do about Captain Thunderbolt. (But whereas Thunderbolt or Ned Kelly become anti-heroes right away, Blak outlaws are remembered by settlers as sad examples, led off the rails from respectable improvement by *white men's vice* or *doomed fate*.)

(What of the generation of European overseers and station hands who, having ducked and weaved through the frontier wars on the squatters' stations, live through Mary's time in New England? Over three or four decades, surviving perpetrators of massacres must be at large amongst town and station communities throughout New South Wales. In the case of the Myall Creek Massacre, seven men are hanged for the murder of thirty Wirrayaraay people in 1838; but four who are originally tried for the murder are let off – including the man, Fleming, who is later deduced to be the ringleader.)

((Fleming hurries to the Hunter Valley and starts a new life. How do he and his accomplices get on with their past, the memory of their acts fading inside station managers' diaries inside family libraries inside archives? Will their neighbours be as frightened of these free criminals as they are of a black man with a gun?))

(((And will Mary take a potshot at Yarrow Creek Tommy, if she sees him on her property? Is she the good pioneer? Or can she forget herself in a second?)))

Terry is back, perfectly unharmed. The woman is already pregnant when he brings her around to Mary's. They've been at Inverell. She has a dead husband, killed on a muster, and five kids of different shades.

It is common in these parts, Mary knows, for a woman with a bullocky husband to take what she can get. Some wives have two or three men on rotation. Some get paid. Mary doesn't say this to Terry, who is stuck on the woman something terrible.

The white horse has wandered away by the time Mary's trespass notice appears in the *Examiner*. She cuts it out and pastes it to the wall inside the front door, as if she wants to remind herself of something.

Mary lies in bed. Dogs are howling very far off, high up in the range; more like a collective humming than a call. The fog has found its way through the slabs and newspaper and hangs above her face. She can hear Maggie already up outside, boiling water in the copper.

A couple of skillion rooms have been tacked onto the hut, one a kitchen and the other for cool storage and where they do the fatty soap and candles. They've replaced the old bark roof with tin; the corrugations direct water down, like the locals did with the leaves on their gunyahs, and she collects it overnight into troughs. Maggie uses the extra water to do laundry for the remaining Chinese bachelors, who exchange the clean clothes for sacks of flour and sugar from town.

It's a long while since Mary has tasted that bush honey. The last time they came through, the old bark sellers said they were going over to the reserve on the river for a while. It was autumn, then; the joeys over this way were nearly shot out for bounty, and the bullocks had smashed the turtle eggs.

A sandy clearing in the jumping arena, a drum of fire. The settler audience, bundled up against the late autumn frost, is in high spirits. They have been eating sweets and inspecting wool samples all day long, flirting and cheering on their cousins' puddings. Terry led his prize bull out of the ring only a couple of hours ago.

One man from the Oban reserve calls the others onto the clearing. The audience surprises itself with a sudden burst of hush. Mary feels embarrassed at the anticipation, like a child.

The roaring flames from the drum light the performers at odd angles, making the White kids in the audience gasp and point at the shadows. They are used to seeing one another in the glow of a slush lamp, but they no longer share campfires like some of their parents did. The reflection of flames on brown faces has become unfamiliar to them.

In the fire Mary sees the mountain gums at night when she looks over Beardy Plain. The image triggers the odour of wild animal fur as it singes over coals. The laughter in her has stopped, and also in the bodies around her.

But as the female performers begin singing in high-pitched voices over the fire, the audience falls into ridiculous giggles and dog howls. Young settler women scream in mock terror. Soon exclamations and then loud conversation. A boy in front of Mary asks his sister what supper was left at home. The performers finish and walk out of the firelight.

A few moments later, the Oban group reappear. The crowd shushes itself again. The performers do a scene of tin miners fighting over a stolen sheep. Mary notices that one of the Oban actors has his face painted white and his shirt stuffed to create a drunkard's paunch, and she catches the joke. The audience's mood shifts from ridicule to relief, a moment of trust extends from the crowd to the performers. Mary feels it bending like a green twig.

I'm having lunch with one of my father's brothers, catching him up on the Mary Cassidy history. He recalls that their grandfather – Mary's grandson – was a member of a minstrel band during the 1920s.

I'd already come across a news clipping from 1901 that mentioned a Miss Cassidy singing at a recital that also featured 'up-to-date nigger minstrels' outside Glen Innes.

I ask my uncle what he thinks the minstrel acts were all about.

He grimaces. 'Were they imitating Aboriginal people?'

I don't answer because I don't know. Or, rather, I don't know if the performing Cassidys knew.

A waiter orbits in. I clutch my plate and she spins away. I'm chewing, chewing.

The Glen Innes cemetery is set on a rise where it gets clipped by the highlands wind. The rose bushes shake and desiccated fragments of grave gifts fly along the grass.

The Cassidys are buried here and there. Mary has a small group of family with her in the Roman Catholics. The mason's design on her headstone is striking: a simple wreath of leaves, gathering a hairy shawl of lichen. I walk around the cemetery trying to piece together a posey from whatever's around. With a scrappy handful of foliage, I twist bark around the stems and lay them on Mary's gravestone. As I stand there, the wind delicately dismembers the posey and flings it away.

There are one or two other people wandering along the rows of colonial graves. Over in the new section, a couple arrives and begins tidying up their loved ones' monuments.

I feel a deep turn in my guts. I'm on fruit and water today, after treating myself at the local steakhouse last night.

I look across the cemetery for a public toilet. I see the caretaker's hut, locked up, in the corner of one boundary. Other than that, no buildings. A short thrill of anxiety runs up between my lungs. The walk back to the southern entrance and the drive back into town would require ten minutes at least.

I casually saunter out of the Cassidy row and back to the northern fence of the cemetery. There's an overgrown nest of hardenbergia looming over the fence like some sort of Green Man, beard dangling onto the lawn.

The couple in the new section are crouched down with their backs to me, working. The fellow tourists are diverted by Presbyterians, pointing and mouthing something under the gust.

I peel down my jeans and squat in the arms of the creeper, looking directly at the gaze of Mary's headstone. The lichen on her stone wreath bristles.

It takes a collective effort to wash Mary's community.
Aspirational mums'n'dads. Mining and jobs. Subdivision.
In 1872 Glen Innes forms a council, which regulates a standard
of municipal living. Those who stay have local kids, local schools
at last –
who was out and in is something to decide.
And although they left brumbies to roam for generations, squatters
and their shepherds pass away, taking the memory of frontier law.

X

It takes state control to achieve 'growing respectability' at home. In the 1880s assimilation policy puts citizens on patrol: itinerancy, theft, alcoholism ~~PTSD~~ are now *the aborigine question*. In fact the real problem is remembering to forget not forgive, since you have to forget yourself to be a patroller. See in 1914 one of my great-grandmothers posts a notice in a Glen Innes newspaper, requesting that her husband be refused the sale of liquor.

X

Those who have survived an apocalypse are resisting
being headcounted at the annual blanket handout
are working in paddocks, mines and kitchens
demanding housing for workers
caring for settler kids
as well as their own
and unknown in
plain sight

by folks who look like me

/ continuing in ways you couldn't see \

It's early evening in late April.

Mary's son, my great-great-grandfather Terence, describes how at this hour of the day, when he and his brother first travelled from western Sydney to Glen Innes, he had played with a clearing full of 'native bears' at the edge of the New England tablelands.

But that was November when the heat was building; now it's still and dry. If I squint, the New England tablelands resemble parts of Ireland for about five seconds. I hear a snort of mirth.

Mary Cassidy was proud of her Gaelic origins in the west of County Clare; she would have recognised the Standing Stones at Glen Innes, the long shadows cast at sunset by their dolmen forms.

I'm afraid of shadows. Is the structure *really* ancient? tourists ask. Was there a great White race here, after all? Or are the stones maybe a bit *Aboriginal*?

The ambiguity is deliberate. Constructed in the late twentieth century as a monument to 'Celtic' settler identity, they're the town's main tourist attraction. They overlook Glen Innes, scabbed all over with plaques dedicated to local individuals, families and Rotary projects. There's an annual Celtic festival centred on the Stones. I am told that under proposal is a 'Celtic village' to give tourists a 'medieval experience'. A local says the Stones represent Celtic-ness that 'brings to mind an ancient way of life, a sense of mystery'.

What is it, to bring to mind? Is it memory, or fantasy? Some say that early European settlers in Australia had so lost touch with their own ancient heritage, they couldn't recognise native crops of unrefined grain and seed.

I'm afraid of mystery. I'm afraid of being imagined into a way of life that isn't mine and wasn't Mary's.

Mary Cassidy's story is of 'friends, neighbours and strangers who live near and far; citizens marked by difference and sameness; people of varying predicaments, capacities and desires'. Someone might correct me. I've tried to construct her story as a form of listening – a story of counter-counter facts – because the alternative is silence, or mystery.

As a midwife she delivered her own grandchildren and other babies in the northern tablelands – at Glencoe and Ben Lomond, fair distances from Glen Innes on horseback or by cart. There were so many women who didn't have their own mothers nearby, alive, or even in Australia. Mary pulled their babies into the consequences of the past.

Relaxed and Comfortable

Risdon Cove, Van Diemen's Land
(1830–1860)

In *The Fabrication of Aboriginal History*, historian Keith Windschuttle rails against a movement of revisionists, who he sees as claiming to be 'their nation's redeemers' and driven by 'white vanity'.

Windschuttle is particularly irked by research of the 1804 massacre at piyura kitina, Risdon Cove. Soldiers and settlers at Lieutenant Bowen's original colony site opened fire on a group of Oyster Bay people approaching a mob of kangaroo. Windschuttle questions claims to the number of Palawa people killed and that the colonists were on the offensive.

He feels that by focusing on a more critical representation of colonists' historical narratives and sources, historians such as Lyndall Ryan and Henry Reynolds have made a dramatic event from what was actually a bland, calm surface.

Windschuttle goads: 'Who among them would want to live in a largely benign, uneventful and moderately successful minor nation? How much more exciting to inhabit a country fatally flawed by, but oblivious to, its own terrible dark past.'

But there's no such binary. Re-reading the past reveals that terrible and dark and flawed acts live right alongside of – *with and within* – the uneventful and benign and oblivious ones.

Remembering history makes us human. This depends upon our ability to understand that we *create* memory; that we go about making monuments, and how we use them in an ongoing way.

Proposing the monument to Tunnerminnerwait and
Maulboyheener
Jim Everett-puralia meenamatta stood up and declared
WE ARE STILL HERE

His kin, Trawlwoolway author Neika Lehman wrote a poem called 'Memorial'. It might be about Tunnerminnerwait and Maulboyheener or about co-existing with your past.

remember two dead men
suspend life to picture the dead
we never think to forget the dead
it is unnatural and suspicious to forget the dead
we are always the dead, living
forget of living
the dead are a form and meaning
we are precariously dead
On top and under the ground
living the dead in love
I am in love with the dead
my ancestors
dead in love,
living my ancestors

I was schooled not to know the dead. This was not extraordinary. I was schooled to forget the unknown. The unknown people and places could not be loved. The ultimate fabrication of history, then, is the one that can't touch us.

In 1832 a convict
bashes one of his master
Richard Cleburne's kiddies.
The penal command puts the
convict on bread and water.

In 1832 Cleburne
witnesses a constable restraining
a convict on the street in Hobart.
Offended by the force being used
Cleburne pushes the constable off.

Cleburne is apprehended.
The public opines in the newspapers:
outrage at the Vandemonian police,
those 'little underlings' of the law.

The law loses. Cleburne, a 'humane christian', is let go.

While I'm writing this
my friends ask me if I am *uncovering terrible things*.

Yes/no.
I am uncovering loops and holes
noting the punished convict, who
once he finishes his bread and his
bondage joins the Governor's payroll

and following the esquire Cleburne, who
abhors the abuse of power and is surrounded by it.

In 1840, my great-great-great-grandfather Richard Cleburne moves his family into their new home at Risdon Cove.

Freshly used Palawa huts, food and artwork are found in southern Tasmania near the Franklin River and at Frenchmans Cap.

Our cannon listening.
The swamp hens listening.
The cove.

Richard Cleburne knows that a massacre took place just a spear's throw from his new home.

It is one of the first things he learned when he arrived in Van Diemen's Land, when it was already a second-hand story. A commission into the Risdon Cove massacre was being brought. Living accounts of the 1804 attack were being stirred. Cleburne noticed that the hoo-ha helped rally public support for the Governor's Black Line campaign in the 1830s.

Governor Arthur's volunteers and military scoured the plains, forests and hills of the island's occupied centre. The Black Line ended two hours' walk from where Cleburne now sits. The military strategists were confident that the strip of hilly bush along the Derwent River was too difficult or too exposed as a safe place for Palawa.

My great-great-great-grandfather has carefully waited nearly twenty years to move upriver, into this place under the hill. He hates the violence of Hobart but he isn't a fool; for a long while, living at Risdon Cove has been considered a death wish for a settler family.

Cleburne has heard about a couple of fresh ambush attacks on farmhands, but they are distant in the north-west of the island. It's been a good five years since Chief Protector Robinson and the governor announced their friendly mission accomplished.

At Risdon Cove, bits of the 1804 massacre site are recycled into new buildings or abandoned to sheep.

So there they sit, the Cleburne family, for their first meal at the Risdon Cove homestead.

The maid listening,
the vegetables listening.

After the stupidity of the Black Line, thinks Cleburne, it was the humane plan that had made sense. The fellows at the Mechanics Institute agreed.

Something itches him; the news of the natives has all but dried up. There is a group of people on an island, not long ago the terror of Van Diemen's Land, and no one in Hobart society has mentioned them for years. That is the way of a goal, Cleburne reasons, but who is on guard? While he likes a self-made man, he has always thought that Robinson walks and talks like an underling.

Cleburne is sitting at my great-great-great-grandfather John Curwen-Walker's place in 1842. Since moving into Risdon Cove a couple of years ago, he spends most Saturday afternoons in his friend's drawing room, looking back at his own house across the river. He considers raising the question with Curwen-Walker but keeps mum.

Early on in Robinson's mission, Curwen-Walker's bank had supported a public account to raise funds for a monument to Robinson. Curwen-Walker had felt it was a sure thing, but the burghers of Hobart would not commit. The banker was puzzled but to Cleburne the reason seemed obvious and he'd told Curwen-Walker as much: nobody knew yet which way the mission would go. What if the builder was put up on a pedestal and then Hobart was stormed by returning natives?

Next, their friend the painter Benjamin Duterrau had begun to lobby for supporters to finance a grand painting of the Chief Protector. This time, though, the silence grew even louder.

'Ben wept for the blacks,' says Curwen-Walker. 'As we all did.' Topping up Cleburne's whiskey, he points to a sketch propped on a sideboard. 'The finished thing's been sitting in his studio for two damn years.'

Cleburne's mouth is ajar. Hadn't Duterrau failed to raise funds for the painting's completion?

'Did it on his own time and pocket, in the end,' explains Curwen-Walker. 'Doesn't make a lick of difference, of course. If nobody wanted it then, they sure don't now. Poor old Ben.'

Cleburne examines the sketch. He watches the figures move. Robinson, Tunnerminnerwait, Maulboyheener, Truganini, and Wurati depart Wybalenna and cross the Bass Strait to Port Phillip. He watches Robinson and Tunnerminnerwait go travelling about the whaling station at Portland taking interviews. He watches Robinson watching one thousand natives at a lake in the sheep country of Port Phillip. Now, Cleburne sees faces from the sketch sitting in a courtroom.

He bites the rim of his tumbler.

'He's not done well, has he? I still say our names ought to be on a roll beside that picture, RC. Snap it up now and put it in the Mechanics. You and I, and a few good dogs all chuck in. It'd give old Ben a real push.'

Cleburne looks from the sketch back to Curwen-Walker, whose tumbler is still full. What is it actually a picture of? Cleburne wants to ask his friend.

'Drink up, old doggie.' Curwen-Walker gently kicks Cleburne's gouty ankle.

That evening, pissed and scrambling at his front door, Cleburne finds his wife and daughters locked inside the house. Their maid from Donegal is sitting with them on the silk chaise, crying.

In 1842, as my great-great-great-grandfathers snore beside the Derwent River, four Palawa people are found living on the west coast of Van Diemen's Land. They include Oyster Bay people from the Coal Valley – the Country behind piyura kitina, Risdon Cove.

They are taken to Wybalenna.

When I was a kid, my mother told me the story of a maid at Richard Cleburne's home by piyura kitina, Risdon Cove.

In my mind's eye I play myself as the young convict woman, resourceful in my panic. In that moment, it seems, anything I am holding will become a weapon.

Later, my mother writes the story down for me. In that version she includes a spear, resting beside the black feet which the maid sees as she looks down from her work beside a hearth.

Had I forgotten that spear from the original telling, or had my mother? The spear changes the story: now, the man has come protected but not with a weapon to use up-close.

I look in the Cleburne homestead: the kitchen fireplace is inside, near a door that opens onto a paved yard. It's possible the encounter begins when the maid is raking ash from the kitchen fireplace, to dump outside.

Or perhaps it occurs when she is building coals outside, to boil river water for washing.

Or maybe the Palawa man walks right into the kitchen.

If the encounter between him and the Cleburne's maid takes place during the early Black War, the warrior might be emboldened – a scout advancing before a group raid. Very few recorded attacks on the lands of the Oyster Bay nation leave settler occupants unharmed, but a couple of times the guerilla fighters spare women.

On the other hand, if the encounter happens during the Governor's Black Line campaign, the man might be seeking sustenance before continuing to slip along timtumili minanya,

Derwent River. After all, people of the Oyster Bay and Big River nations are repeatedly passing through the Line unnoticed.

Whatever the case, the Palawa man either does not hesitate to cross between spaces – a proprietor coming to turf out trespassers – or he has reason to put himself in great danger by approaching the house.

But I have changed the story again.
My mother never mentions the sex of the feet, so why am I writing 'he'?
The story taught me.
And there is a big limb missing from this tree. I have only just noticed it.

Richard Cleburne's family don't move into their Risdon Cove homestead until the early 1840s. Now, the guerilla leader Tongerlongeter is dead; the fight for Van Diemen's Land is believed by most settlers to be over; the 'desert island' prison of Wybalenna is drifting out of mind. By now, Robinson has transferred himself to Chief Protector for Aborigines in Port Phillip; his companions Maulboyheener and Tunnerminnerwait are preparing to be executed.
Our story of the maid, her coals, the feet and their spear must be happening *after* forty years of attempted genocide and organised resistance.
The person who comes to Cleburne's house is, according to the state, the gentry, the underlings and the media, no longer supposed to exist. They are supposed to belong in a painting.

Why hadn't I seen that before?
   The painting blinded me.

The survivors of Wybalenna and the women excused by Port Phillip law are moved to a reserve south of Hobart, promoted as 'the sole survivors of the Black population of Tasmania'.

Robinson returns himself to England. He closes the colonial compartments of his mind.

Richard Cleburne has no intention of leaving the colony.

He buys the nearby ferry house and launches a public boat service across the Derwent. Day-trippers from Hobart load their carts on and tour about the old massacre site at Risdon Cove. Cleburne pours the whiskeys now.

In 1855 he accepts an invitation to the Governor's inspection party to see the Famous Last Tasmanians on their reserve. Staying at the rear of the group, nodding and smiling, he can hardly believe these old women in knitted caps and cardigans are the naked, shorn-haired ones in Benjamin Duterrau's painting.

Afterwards, as he still does most Saturday afternoons, Cleburne parks himself in John Curwen-Walker's drawing room. The two neighbours have become sort of brothers since their children married one another. Cleburne gazes up at the strange image as he drinks the top off his memory.

After years of going on about it, after old Ben is dead and gone, Curwen-Walker himself has bought *The Conciliation*.

For his friend, supposes Cleburne, it's a nostalgic piece. These days it looks like a memorial to another time. When they were all trying not to look at the edges of the picture or into its eyes.

'The more peaceful and less penal this *Tasmania* becomes, the less profitable,' jokes John Curwen-Walker to his mates.

Of course, he is not joking. In 1862, he packs up and heads to the land of wool and gold: *Victoria*. The contents of his house are listed for auction.

On the advertised day Richard Cleburne crosses the Derwent and walks sadly through the familiar, now abandoned rooms.

In the drawing room, which echoes as furniture is carried out around him, he sits down on his favourite armchair.

The Conciliation looks.

What is it a picture of, now, twenty years since Robinson's mission?

The next day, the picture arrives at the house under the hill at Risdon Cove.

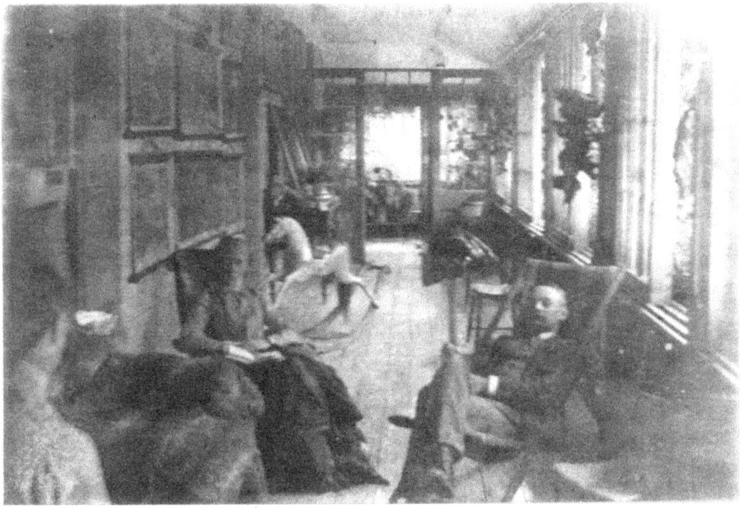

The daughters of Richard Cleburne have one task in life: to practice the art of landscape.

My great-great-aunts, Emma and Louisa Cleburne and their sisters, produce picture after picture of their childhood home, unpeopled.

Here's one vision. Mount Direction provides a sublime horizon. Its foothills gently bed down sheep and tiny vacant houses. A middle ground is composed of still waters on the Derwent River. An unmanned barque skids behind the foreground; casuarinas on rocky banks.

Here, a more domestic pastoral: the back gate of the Cleburne house, a shepherd and dog herding past, the rooftop and orchard otherwise silent.

And another, from further beyond the gate: the oldest chimney in Van Diemen's Land, a romantic ruin of the first colony at Risdon Cove. Tall as a witness.

I go further back – deeper into the cove. Before the Cleburne family's arrival, before their memory. Wading into a history that advances, recedes, darkens and brightens.

The lagoon behind timtumili minanya, Derwent River is filled with soft rushes. A pair of black swans drifts below farms bordered by bush. After I pass the Cleburne homestead and round the hill behind it, I spot a stone ford crossing the marsh at the edge of the lagoon. A gentle, unenclosed hamlet, very like the frontier fringe I imagined as a child.

The Tasmanian Aboriginal Centre (TAC) has renamed Risdon Cove *piyura kitina*. In palawa kani, a reconstructed language of Tasmanian Aboriginal people, this means 'little native hens'. I can see them, pecking and jogging about on the grass beside the creek that hugs the back of the hillside. The name recalls the peacefulness of the site, its watery element and fragility, its regeneration.

The parking lot of the TAC cultural centre is separated into two sections: for Palawa community using the TAC centre, which is busy with several cars, and for those visiting the monument. I sit in the visitors' section, facing two giant pyramids set within the cove, built in the late seventies as part of a public reserve, and now occupied by the TAC's children's centre and cultural centre. They are shiny and self-contained, established.

'The laughter of our children at this place today is our strongest remedy against the brutalities of its past,' the TAC states.

Its CEO, Heather Sculthorpe, insists that a process of truth and reconciliation, treaty dialogue and community engagement must be undertaken by the Tasmanian state and its institutions, before we 'walk happily on together'. This process seems to be slowly taking place. To demand anything else yet, says Sculthorpe, is to demand an 'assimilation agenda'.

A moribund obelisk, monument to the original colony where the 1804 massacre took place, sits gloomily in the shadow of the pyramids. If you want to get there, you have to pick your way across the lawn of the cultural centre and walk past the crêche around the side of the front pyramid. You can always be seen through its glass walls, reflecting your image back at you.

In 1804, moments before the massacre at Risdon Cove began, a freed convict named Edward White saw hundreds of Oyster Bay kangaroo hunters coming down the valley towards this estuary. He said, 'they looked at me with all their eyes'.

I'm sitting in the dining room of the Cleburne house. Over there is where his daughters, the Misses Cleburne, sketched. Here, is where the *The Conciliation* stood.

My husband and I were married out there, in the courtyard, where black feet walked before and after the Cleburnes arrived.

The owners of the house, David and Penelope, were our witnesses. I ask David what it's like living so close to a massacre site. 'No one says *anything*' in the settler neighbourhood about it, he reckons.

It was the ecological disruption caused by Cleburne's causeway that initially led David into the cove's history. Cleburne built up the causeway across the cove's mouth, to access his river punt. The result was a silted lagoon. Turns out the marsh I saw on my way isn't a great example of a preserved waterway; the flow of the estuary was ruined.

It's as though the causeway also sealed off the easy flow of information about what had happened behind it.

David admits that he'd never heard of the massacre at piyura kitina until he began researching the history of the house. Recently, he found out about Lyndall Ryan's massacre map. When he looked at the map of Australia and saw a dot over 'Risdon Cove', he realised that the site behind his home is a big deal.

To David, who has driven past piyura kitina 'thousands of times' and visited the monument to the colony that participated in massacre, the TAC's use of the space tells a story. 'The monumental scale of what happened there,' he spreads his hands, 'was violence caused by whites. Our sense of the place needs reframing.'

Historian Lyndall Ryan argues for a memorial somewhere to acknowledge the Black Wars of lutruwita, Tasmania, the deaths on both sides. Artist Julie Gough has spent years creating memorials to kin on Country, and reconstructing traumatic sites like the retired statue of William Crowther in nipaluna, Hobart.

In the same spirit, and although he understands why settler access is delimited, David looks forward to a time when the 'healing' at piyura kitina can be shared.

Debates and campaigns around the recognition of Tasmanian Aboriginal identity and language are ongoing, and painful for many. As an outsider it's enough for me to notice that 'some draw strength from a narrative of survival and others grieve at being written out of the story'. Such is the legacy of attempted division and conquest.

And I'm also reminded by artworks like Gough's that survival is an inadequate way of seeing continuing culture and peoples. To David, the site of the first colony, its massacre and its reclaiming isn't confrontational. 'It's like someone with their back turned to you,' David says, 'concentrating on something you can't see.'

We Tell Him All the Long Words

piyura kitina, Risdon Cove
(1860–1940)

```
Richard Cleburne – Harriet Beauvais                    |
              |                                        |
     _____                               |
     |      |         |                                |
   Louisa Emma     Alice – Henry Curwen-Walker    John H. Hansbrough – –
                         |
                         |
                         |
                         |
```

The Conciliation goes uninterrupted for a long time after Richard
Cleburne's death. 'The canvas...has been standing face to the wall
on the floor in their house as long as many living can remember.'

The picture is a medium, it transfers

more than a backdrop. Feel it?

When you think about the objects
you live with, they're like tones
of light on a wall / the angle of a tree
through a window. Marking routines

that make you appear
larger than   Even after

years of passing them by
you still haven't noticed the most obvious detail.

The Cleburne women are snoozing on the verandah after lunch.

Below, the Derwent River pulses.

Hobart smirks in the distance.

The women reach out their arms in sleep.

The man turns away. He has flipped the painting to face the room. What is it saying? Its composition like a stageplay; his eye roves.

These Palawa don't look like any people of colour that John Harrison Hansbrough has known. They're grey, like mortar. It's as though their skin has faded. Bare bellies and breasts are dull. The artist has made their eyes stare keenly from spherical heads. Smaller faces, looking over a hillock, belong in another scene.

Behind them the clouds keep moving over red spears. The animals have crude, scratchy feet. Light reflects off the White man Robinson's calico crotch, which is being sniffed by a dog. The shell necklaces sparkle; apart from the dog's snout, they are the only lively thing.

It looks to John like that *Penn's Treaty* picture, which he saw badly printed in the hotel lobby he worked back in DC. The pointing, the looking, the White man's fabric.

The women don't wake up. Their flesh is crumpled linen.

He sits down to write.

Misses Emma and Louisa Cleburne
their widowed mother, Harriet
live on for over fifty years
in a museum of colonial cargo –

Irish silver and war ships' cannon
framed and rolled paintings, china
antique books and marsupial furs
the rotted Confederate hulk by the jetty.

In the 1890s someone interrupts the lull of that unmanned vessel, the house under the hill.

...the Misses Cleburne wore white gloves and would brush their fingers along the skirting boards to make sure there was no dust. Excitingly, they employed a Negro servant called Hansborough [sic], who wore a suit and top hat and white gloves, and rode a bicycle, though then he tied paper bags around his trousers to stop them getting dirty. The bicycle was ancient, and he could only stop it by running into a tree. The Misses Cleburne relied heavily on him, and when they were old and feeble he slept on the end of their bed. He was an important part of the little Risdon community, for he recited poetry at dances, and added a touch of rare glamour – his sister was a 'beauty doctor' in America. How Hansborough ended up in Risdon on the other side of the world is a complete mystery.

All the gloves in the world can't hide the White family's imprint on this *mystery*.
    Mystery is like weird landscapes, vanished lands and dying races. It prefers to be uninhabited.

I'll start again, louder this time.

John Harrison Hansbrough is remembered and denied. The accounts of him I grew up with were mementos. Of us: the Cleburne descendants. He joins the curiosities of confected belonging: the stuff of inheritance.

As I reread the account of John's 'rare glamour', it seems that the family always viewed him this way. He is an addition to the collection, a frisson; an edge. They hold 'the capacity of the exhibitor to control and exhibit'.

They hold the capacity to decide what belongs inside and out. If their own white gloves are a way of highlighting the dirt of servitude, John's white gloves are a uniform to reflect his employers' status.

Emma and Louisa Cleburne want to be seen. They like to bathe in the Derwent River, where John delivers them boiled water. They like contrasts. Black hands, White feet.

Maybe the Misses Cleburne can tolerate these dissonant images because they amount to one image, one idea: themselves. Tolerance, writes Ghassan Hage, is 'emitted by people who fantasise that it is up to them'. They want to be seen bestowing it. Tolerance isn't asked for, after all, it's given.

I find it wide awake in the Cleburne family archive:

Hansbrough...loyally / and with tact, supported the Misses Emma and Louisa when they were without other immediate protection... [He] treated the family with delicate respect. Younger members enjoyed trips to the Richmond Hotel in Hobart, with Hansbrough on the box, or by cart round the Mount, with him cooking onions on the way.

John sounds like everyone's favourite uncle; the ones the kids run to when there's a family gathering. But I trace the line – fine yet firm, around his shape. Loyal, tactful, supportive, protective, respectful. John is an adjective.

The archive loves mystery. It glances then looks away.

I've stuck two photographs of John Hansbrough on the wall before me. In one, he stands on the crest of a road in 1910. Pushing the infamous bike, he wears a resourcefully fashioned rucksack made from a burlap bag tied with string across his chest.

Gawking tells me very little. I note the angle of his hat. I note the dry, pale gravel on the slope. And I will him to blink.

John was born in 1860, near Stevensburg, Virginia. Before leaving the USA he was a farmer at nearby Brandy Station.

He arrived in Australia in 1894.

Description of applicant:

Age: 42 years
Height: 5 feet 5 inches
Forehead: Straight
Eyes: Dark
Nose: Large
Mouth: Large
Chin: Medium
Hair: Black
Complexion: Dark
Face: Full

In 1903 he applied for proof of his USA citizenship because of the increasingly strict immigration laws of a White Australia. The application was an agreement that John Harrison Hansbrough would return to the USA by 1905, and that his father was a 'loyal' citizen of the Union.

John is between the lines.

John is

before, during and after the White family.

In histories of the Confederate South, the Hansbrough families of Virginia are slave owners. A namesake of John Hansbrough frees all his human chattels. A slave of Blucher W. Hansbrough, Charles Nalle famously escapes with Harriet Tubman's assistance.

It's possible that Blucher also owns John's mother, a slave named Lucy. Lucy and baby John may be gifted by Blucher to his daughter, Elizabeth, in 1860. John may have several siblings including some who relocate to Washington DC between 1880 and 1920.

Perhaps John's mother is instead owned by George W. Hansbrough, a Confederate soldier. Although a slave owner, George W. becomes a reporter to the Virginia Supreme Court under the Readjustor Party, a bi-racial party that seeks to redistribute the power of elite planters after the Civil War.

Records of the Hansbrough slave women are virtually non-existent. Slave marriages, births and deaths are rarely recorded by their households unless an owner is implicated; and slave registers are typically lists of first names only.

Like Edward Ball says of his family tree in *Slaves in the Family*, 'On one side stood the ancestors, vivid, serene, proud; on the other their slaves, anonymous, taboo, half human' despite their entangled lives.

When I was younger, something about the family's name for John annoyed me. *Hansbrough* or *Hans* said my Nan and my mother and the archival accounts. It was the false familiarity I found irritating and yet, when we use these names generations later, we are keeping alive a Confederate legacy that sought to forget the intimacy of John.

The names on registers of African American slaves are childish, one word and often parodic. I find this naming culture also in explorers' and station owners' monikers for First Nations guides and workers in Australia. Chief Protector Robinson does something similar when he renames the residents of Wybalenna with pet names, like Jack or Napoleon instead of Tunnerminnerwait.

I Google photos of John's birthplace. Stevensburg is now gently sloping, pastoral land.

In shots from the Civil War, however, there are mud, railroad construction and groups of disarrayed men.

John is a toddler. Hansbrough's Ridge, which hosts the largest cavalry battle of the war, the Battle of Brandy Station, is located nearby. Crops and forests around Stevensburg are pillaged by the troop camps, locals go hungry or flee northward out of the chaos. Soon, Unionist parties will enter the big houses, looting and declaring the slaves freed.

As John grows up, his older family and community members of emancipated slaves migrate northwards, leaving the South in search of work. Interracial slaver households divide; Whites get whiter.

I am surprised to find that John has more than one option before him, as a young man. He might become a sharecropper on the same plantation, Brandy Station, at which his family were formerly enslaved. He might, as his sister-in-law in Washington DC later claimed he did, go to a Black college in Virginia or interstate.

Often a Southern Black family will send one offspring north, for better opportunities. Done with farming in the depressed South, John may move to Chicago, where the census records a man of colour named John H. Hansbrough employed as a bellman in 1888 and 1892.

In these northern cities, though, rejection from work comes as a shock to many African Americans from the South. No longer slaves, they are now no longer permitted to be in the company of Whites. Something is circling.

Jim Crow laws begin to obstruct African American progress. The 1890s is the peak period of lynchings in the USA.

I lose sight of John in the crowd. It seems he has bought, as Langston Hughes put it, a 'One-Way Ticket':

I pick up my life
And take it away
On a one-way ticket –
Gone up North,
Gone out West,
Gone!

The news app is running live updates. I watch
tens of thousands marching across American cities to protest
another African American murder at the hands of police. A week
later, like a canopy fire, the protests will leap

and the Australian protests will be more peaceful than in the USA,
but they are fueled by rage over deaths in custody and cultural
dispossession, a rage long burning all around the continent, and
for a moment it feels as if this collective recognition of related
trauma is the only thing that holds Australia together.

In 1894 John arrives in Tasmania. He is in his mid-thirties, the same age as I am when I uncover his story.

He finds work immediately with a pair of unmarried women, Emma and Louisa Cleburne at Risdon Cove.

They are now past middle age; one blind, the other deaf. They pay John to do all the duties of a live-in servant except maid's work of cooking and cleaning. There is no set job description; as in Southern planters' households, men in his line of work are 'butlers, outside caretakers, chauffeurs, footmen, furnace men, coal men, handymen, and housemen'.

He is, of course, something more to the Cleburnes. Although they never say it in so many words, he is *excitingly* different from anything else in the house under the hill.

It wasn't always like this. Before Federation and White Australia policy, Tasmania had encountered difference more commonly. Non-Indigenous people of colour were part of the international maritime port of Hobart since Richard Cleburne's arrival in the 1820s, and much earlier through whaling and expedition shipping. Caribbean and African American men were not unusual on the Victorian goldfields, either.

But when John arrives, there is also something circling here. The majority population has tipped towards Anglo-Celtic, with at least one generation Australian-born. Before you can say *please explain*, newspapers, advertising and then government are linking minorities and particularly people of colour to intemperance, vice, pestilence, swarming, ghettos, queue-jumping, terrorism, gangs, contagion.

Coinciding with vigorous assimilation of First Nations people, White Australia is forgetting itself.

African American performers and boxers like Jack Johnson tour some Australian cities, but they are not what most European settlers of the 1890s think of when they think of the African diaspora. And think is what they do, because seeing and knowing is becoming less common. The cartoon of the blackface minstrel is how White suburban audiences form an idea of a *black* identity.

Originally, in Europe minstrelsy simply meant travelling musicians. But in nineteenth and twentieth century America and Australia the genre is synonymous with blackface. Blackface minstrelsy is familiar to Australian cities and towns when John begins working for the Cleburnes. Close to Risdon, the Hobart Amateur Minstrels troupe are performing weekly from the 1890s up until World War I. Various minstrel shows will continue in Hobart until 1982.

I might never know whether John chooses his uniform in those early days of his employment. The description of his outfit in the family archive depicts not only the formal suit and top hat of a slave coachman; it's also the clothing of someone in performance, an entertainer and an eccentric, the American 'stage negro'.

In the Tasmanian Archives there's a scrapbook from the Cleburne family. It seems to be from the 1880s or 1890s, so it might've belonged to Misses Emma and Louisa.

I imagine the sisters filling their long afternoons. Their dining room overlooks a lawn with a sundial, sloping gently down into the river where it enters the cove. The site of the 1804 massacre is about 800 metres behind them.

First they draw the shells they've collected from the river's edge, where they went bathing. Just once, Emma sketches the back of Louisa playing piano. They don't sketch their elderly mother, Harriet, who has been wheeled out onto the covered verandah in her reclining chair.

At some point a camera fixes one of the sisters, sitting on the verandah. Some of the household museum can be seen around and behind her. A framed painting is visible in the background of the photo, propped up on a sideboard or chest. It seems to have a luminous figure at its centre but it looks too small to be *The Conciliation*. Beside Miss Cleburne reclines a young male visitor – their dissipated brother, perhaps, or a Curwen-Walker in-law. In his fist, he is holding a hatchet.

Next, the Misses Cleburne do their scrapbook. They use a quarto book with big blank pages. They favour poems, stanzas and sometimes whole passages. Around the verses they stick illustrations torn from greeting cards, ladies' journals and packaging. They collect, compulsively. Any slip of blank paper is covered. Romance, satire, domestic humour, pictures of babies, puppies and maidens, ribald and heroic stories.

On the weekend John takes them over to Hobart where they pick up their mail subscriptions.

Their taste is a sort of channel-surfing. They like it all. Pasted sideways down one page of the book is a sliver of *Othello*:

I'll see before I doubt,
when I doubt, prove.

But they don't like that painting of Robinson and the natives that stands in the corner. Not enough, at least, to hang it; not even to face it.

While the Misses collect their mail at the GPO
John secures the trap and walks around the corner
to the front desk at the Hobart *Mercury*.

He has never been 'a complete mystery'.
It's just that no one seems to ask
how John fills his short afternoons.

All they must do is read the newspaper
to find his steady gaze on the near and far:
donations to war charities and international aid;
recitations at meetings and elocution championships.
('A fair voice,' note the judges, 'but needed more emphasis.')

Constructing his own archive
he delivers a letter to the editor.

[Coloured people] are to be found in all walks of life as a civilised
and highly cultivated people. They are in fact giving the lie to the
slanderer, and…will now long stand erect before God and man and
demand justice, equal rights, and recognition among the great
nations of the earth.
Yours, etc
John H. Hansbrough

John even manages to interject in the adjectival Cleburne family archive. In an anecdote jotted down for posterity, another descendent of my great-great-great-grandfather Richard Cleburne comes close to capturing the domestic voice of the 'Negro servant'.

John, goes the scene, has planned a trip to Melbourne during World War I. The Misses Cleburne implore him not to leave them unattended. John replies that he will be blamed if anything happens to the women whether he is there or not, and so he might as well go. (Ouch.)

In this second-hand or even third-hand retort, he can tell us so much. And yet my great-great aunts seem able to convey almost nothing about him even with a torrent of speech and a scribe at hand. At the end of World War I, a local busybody visited 'the house under the hill' at Risdon Cove. Writing it up in her memoir, she thinly disguises Misses Emma and Louisa Cleburne as 'Ellen and Letty Clissold'. They tell her all about their 'aboriginal' employee:

...who worked outside in the daytime, and in the evening read the paper and other things aloud to them. 'Of course,' explained Miss Ellen, 'we tell him all the long words and he is able to read the short ones quite well.' 'Though it is a pity,' ejaculated Miss Letty, 'that he is so disloyal! A great pity that he is so disloyal!'

That the Misses Cleburne might have truly believed the man who lived with them for thirty years was 'aboriginal' speaks for itself. Only slightly more disturbing is the possibility that they knew he was African American but made a social pretense of not caring, or telling, the difference.

In the 1880s and 1890s, 'the foundation narrative of the new nation promulgated an uncomplicated racial divide' between Anglo-Celtic settlers and everyone else. 'In this narrative, any black individual...could only be understood as the despised and excluded other'.

The Cleburnes' habit of denial didn't stop with John's heritage. Their blaming of his presence and absence, the insinuations of his illiteracy and disloyalty, start to build a picture of a pathology.

It is plain to see how
he speaks for himself
in black and white.

   'I belong to the United States –

It is 1896
he is thirty-six years
on Earth and two years
in Tasmania, and this
is his second letter to the editor.

   and therefore speak from personal knowledge'.

About the letters and other activities
no one else in the household knows, or

   if Chancellor Bismarck says 'the negro was intended for a very different destiny from that of the white race of mankind' –

they wished they didn't and so
they don't

   – then John says he's 'either a defamatory liar or an idiot'.

When John reads the newspaper aloud
to the Misses in the evenings
does he perform or does he hide?

When he recites the scramble for Africa for the women
does he pause to share how in Culpeper County,
he heard the bizarre treatise of one Thornton Stringfellow,
Pastor of the Stevensburg Baptist Church of Virginia
who preached that keeping slaves was a Christian act
of holy, legal and merciful qualities just as in the Old Testament?

In 1896 and every other year of letters
he never reveals the colour of his personal knowledge.
He is passing in print, but maybe he is also passing aloud
to these White women

so that he can look back
between the lines at them

   a way of speaking to the future, being the present.

A letter to the editor is a democratic exercise, and in John's case, an act of civic responsibility.

In the USA the end of slavery is being talked about as a national tragedy, a wasted opportunity: 'Between 1865 and 1877, the Negro had proven himself completely unfit for the responsibilities of democratic citizenship'. Australia's federal fathers are listening very closely to Theodore Roosevelt as he searches to advance the 'progress of English peoples in the New World'.

Tasmanian newspapers in the first decade of John's migration are terrified of a 'piebald' Australia. In the 1890s, Hobart's *Mercury* carry a fair report on 'Negro Disenfranchisement' in South Carolina, but as the century turns the 'coloured difficulty' in Oklahoma is described in local media as a 'fiendish' threat; until lynchings and Klan activities are relayed quite neutrally, often sympathetically, in the Australian press.

African American media is watching from a distance. It sees First Nations and Pacific Islander slavery here, and racist immigration and labour policy when most Australians cannot.

John is watching close-up.

Once he wrote that he 'belonged'
to the USA but when in his mid-forties
he is pressed by immigration law to return

John is busy.
In 1903 he goes to the Hobart Town Hall
to see Edmund Barton address the public.

Finding a space towards the front of the room (the hats!)
J.H. Hansbrough listens closely and notes.

When [Barton] began to speak on the subject of a White Australia
and kanaka labour, he seemed to think he had reached a pinnacle
on which he must flap his wings and crow...[Barton] takes great
glory unto himself for having established a White Australia policy...
appealing to the prejudice of his audience.

John stays until the end looking all the while
at the Prime Minister

'selfish and unscrupulous'

because a White audience is a scared audience.
A White Crow is amongst us.

A Crow, wrote John, to 'fill the breasts of the ignorant with a vain, haughty pride'. A Crow to demonise the Pacific Islander slave who 'did not come here of his own accord, and since he has been here has done nothing meaner than hard work'.

A Crow to cack on 'our own beautiful little island'.

John has been 'sojourning' in Hobart for eight years and counting.

'My being is "known" by whites
before my arrival,' writes George Yancy.
'I reside in a fixed place, always
already waiting for me. In short, then, I exist ahead
of myself.'

By residing in Hobart, out of place
John puts the question
of his being to others.
The sojourner who stays
too long in Australia provokes
a 'bigotry lurking deeper within
the popular mind'.

His thinking seemed to be going
there in his third letter, in 1905:
where once he wrote in terms of savages
and civilised, by now he articulates a global
White conspiracy.

He is the same age as A.M. Fernando,
perhaps he knows that he's mistaken
as Aboriginal. And yet he never mentions
the First Nations of the place he decides to 'belong'.

After fifteen years in Tasmania
John is naturalised –
exempt from the dreaded Dictation Test.
No longer at risk of his sojourn being denied
he takes a trip to the USA in 1909.

Maybe he goes to DC, maybe
separate restrooms, restaurants, separate justice
maybe to Brandy Station the empty fields
is already known and matters even less than at home.
Maybe he writes more, radically disloyal
to those who are already waiting for him
to return to his little island.

The memoirist visits the Cleburne homestead again, in the 1920s. She looks over the Derwent to the zinc works, a satanic industrial complex on the pastoral landscape of the riverbank beneath John Curwen-Walker's old patch. And then

Hastily turning my back on the grim vision, I lifted the rusty latch and crossed the withered lawn, where the bell still hung, and the sundial still marked the passing of the silent hours. The door on to the veranda was open, and the scent of the white jasmine filled the air. The house was silent, and no one answered my gentle knocking, or moved within when I ventured inside the shabby passage. So I retraced my steps, and, guided by a tapping sound among the deserted out-houses at the back, I came upon an old aboriginal, who was evidently the disloyal but still faithful servant, cutting up a small log for firewood. He smiled widely and…brought me back to the veranda…

Still 'a'boriginal, still disloyal, still faithful (make up your mind), John is in his sixties. Overseeing those silent scraps of empire adrift on the passage of his own time.

In Alex Haley's *Roots*, the formerly enslaved Chicken George returns to the home of his 'massa' to retrieve his promised certificate of freedom, only to find Massa Lea bereft, confused and drunk.

Inside the Cleburne house, the memoirist finds the surviving mistress half-sensible on a daybed, no longer capable of control.

John is master of this house. Witnessing the decay of the heirlooms and their bewildered inheritor, is his gaze.

I have another photo of John, taken about this time. He has a crop of non-greying hair, a waistcoat and jacket, empty-handed. His expression is less relaxed than in the other portrait; quizzical, questioning the intentions of the camera. The picket fence behind him is lined with mesh to stop pests. The direction he's facing is towards the back of the house, towards the Risdon Cove monument. The shadow that falls is his own

horizon

After the death of the last Miss Cleburne, my mother's father inherits the house and its contents.

As a boy from Ballarat, he had been sent there for holidays; he was one of the kids John had taken on coach rides. At some point after he'd married Nan, though, my grandfather stopped visiting Risdon Cove.

For another twenty years, John stays on there. The farmland of the property is divided and sold. The new neighbours, writes John to my mother's father, 'treat me Royal'.

His letters to my grandfather in Ballarat are warm but entirely concerned with the little world of the property. John invites the Curwen-Walkers to come stay. He reports on where particular items might be moved to, how the new farmer is, what the place looks like. He's performing the role of caretaker carefully. Loyal, respectful, supportive, delicate, etc., etc.

How different these private letters are to the ones John wrote to the editor of the *Mercury*. But once again, he asserts himself in ways that are easy for me to miss. My family always referred to him as Hans or Hansbrough, but to my mother's father he signs his letters just as he does publicly, 'J.H. Hansbrough' or 'John H. Hansbrough'. For a former enslaved person, or in John's case, an enslaved infant, '[t]aking one's own name…was a potent gesture of self-emancipation'. It is how he saw himself.

In one of these letters, he describes how visitors come to see the house and how he guides them through its history and 'old relicks'. When he leads these tours, does he mention the history of the cove before the house arrived?

Does he mention the old family story of a Palawa person returning? Does he call the visitors over to look at the painting that the old women had covered up? The eyes of Truganini and Maulboyheener.

Does he ask the people what it means to them? Does he tell them what he thinks it means?

Whether or not Nan ever meets *The Conciliation* face to face, she does meet John. He brings himself to Ballarat, to the home of my grandfather. He crosses the distance that the family would prefer to maintain.

She will recall his accent and singing voice, and his haircare regimen. She will remember that John had called my grandfather 'Massa' and had confided to her that the boy who came to visit Risdon Cove was lazy.

I don't know if my Nan is still employed as housekeeper to my grandfather then, or if she has already become his wife. Do she and John together see and know things about this family that it can't see? Or is she still a White woman and he a Black man? He is the same age as her German grandfather, Herman Anders; can she see John as kin?

My grandfather has John sleep in the toolshed.

X

John is eighty-five when he dies in Hobart, leaving
the house at Risdon Cove unoccupied. Imagine
the pile of 'relicks' being carried out, heaping up
bystanders to supremacy.

My mother's father must decide what to do with that white elephant, *The Conciliation*.

He will spend the next fifteen years trying to squeeze the Tasmanian Museum and Art Gallery (TMAG) for his desired price. He refuses the institution's request to donate the picture and have his name displayed on a plaque. Instead, he waits. 'Have you unearthed some properly patriotic man (with a soul) who wishes to retain the Conciliation picture for your gallery?' he pushes the director.

Once again, it seems the painting asks a price that can't be met – and yet. It is sticky. Eventually, and at the expense of installing toilets, TMAG negotiates to pay.

X

When her father was dying, recalls my mother, he invited her to pick what she wanted from her childhood home in Ballarat.

He had furnished it with plenty of the antiques and heirlooms from Risdon Cove. My mother asked him to choose what she could have. He selected a silver fish slice and a pair of serving spoons chased with the Cleburne crest. His gesture was, she says, 'like giving trinkets to the natives'.

X

John is not a picture or a chased spoon
he doesn't have a *meaning*.

And I can't help but read him
as a chapter in the story a limb on the family tree
like 'the fact that you are reading subtitles
during a foreign film fades from your awareness,
yet their message still dictates how you see
what's happening'.

In the story, he is intolerable:
witness to things that should have been disremembered.

He masters the compassion of a *humane Christian*
for White sickness.

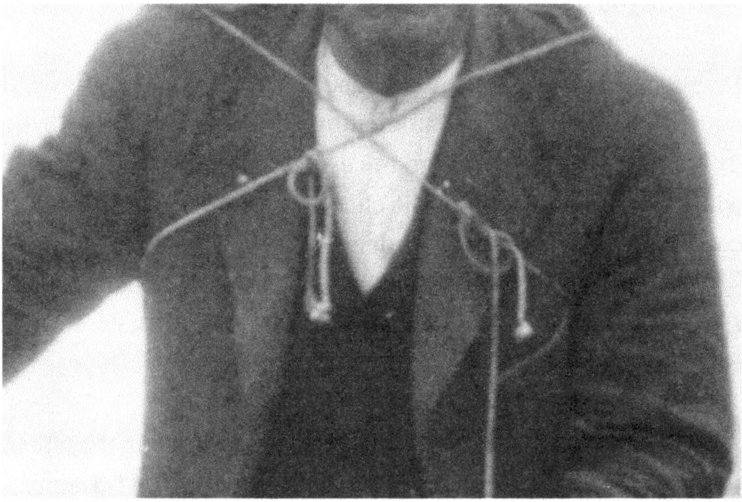

'Why are you here?'

In 1904, between letters to the newspaper, John Hansbrough attends the unveiling of the monument at Risdon Cove. Or he drives the Misses Cleburne to the event and then goes for a walk while he waits. Or he hears the cheers and fanfare coming up the cove as he works in the yard under the hill.

A stone obelisk, the monument marks the centenary of Van Diemen's Land's first British colony. Its shadow spells out the centenary of the colony's first genocidal massacre.

Amateur local historian Reg Watson has been watching the fate of the monument for many years, and campaigning for the Tasmanian Aboriginal Centre to be held accountable for its maintenance. For Reg, the site of Lieutenant Bowen's colony is important nationally and 'certainly the most important one in Tasmania'. When the monument was unveiled 'in 1904 Tasmania was very much part of the British Empire', he points out, having recently sent troops to the South African War. It would have been 'the natural thing to do' to celebrate that relationship, says Reg. Thousands of people were there, bands, military, navy and VIPs, the Premier and Governor. The monument was a signal of their present condition, he explains, because 'Tasmania had thrown off the serious and difficult conditions of early settlement.'

But Tasmania has another, parallel life happening in 1904. A serious and difficult one. The Royal Society of Tasmania articulates Truganini's remains into a skeleton and mounts it at the TMAG for public display. An African American resident of Hobart writes a public letter shaming the Prime Minister for his views on black slave labour in Australia.

This double life, this dissonance of the settler colonial state, doesn't end. In 1978, Tasmania makes a show of the 150th anniversary of the Risdon Cove invasion. Again, Reg says, the public was 'appreciative' of the monument.

In 1978, a new documentary called *The Last Tasmanian* is debated by Palawa community and historians as to its notions of Palawa extermination. An Aboriginal Parliament tent is pitched in Hobart to organise support for local land rights. It's hard for settlers to hold these facts together.

Nowadays, Reg believes that the monument retains its currency for 'descendants of the Bowen settlement'.

Is it time, as David Rieff has suggested, for that currency to be actively forgotten by contemporary local society; time for new memories to be represented by the living?

Ruptures in the smooth culture of denial are happening. On the day that the state hands over Risdon Cove to the TAC in 1995, members of the Palawa community spray red paint over the monument. Some say it is an act of public catharsis. Plaques are created by the TAC to circle the obelisk, narrating the Risdon Cove massacre and the history of Palawa resistance. Nearby, twentieth century replicas and a few remaining artefacts from the colony are vandalised or left to fall apart.

As they fracture into the soil, they release questions like rubble.

Can a monument logically continue to mean the same thing for one hundred years?

Can anything possibly be the most important site in lutruwita, Tasmania?

Who was 'the public' in 1904? Who is it now?

Is the public the same as the state? Is the public everybody in sight in one place at one moment of time? Or is it everyone with a local address?

And who are the descendants of the Bowen colony? Are they cultural or biological? Are they Tasmanian or Australian, or neither?

Reg acknowledges the complexity of such 'politics' but prefers to keep it separate from 'historical fact'. For him, iconoclasm is just denial. It's an interesting point, and in fact it agrees with remarks made from a different standpoint by First Nations truth-telling advocates such as Senator Lidia Thorpe.

There is no use for moral superiority in questioning historical communities and individuals. But, for me, the distinction between politics and fact is a live question when the history of this country has been so very eventful. We need politics to deal with the facts. The record, in other words, is still up for witness, consensus, revision.

I don't feel that a portion of society can, as Reg puts it, 'throw off' difficulties such as racial inequality or attempted genocide, like chucking a warm can of Bundy out of a moving car. Of course, it can do so volitionally, but I'm concerned with the bodies and brains of each of us. If society is an ecology, then nothing disappears. 'The public' is absorbing and consuming and reacting. A portion of society might comfortably drive on for a while – until the hot, sticky can comes flying back through the window.

This is going to hurt. When I look at images of the stones gashed with red paint, it's distressing but I see a monument that looks alive, like my history. It's violent but it looks intentional, like inhabitation. It looks true.

The monument to Bowen and the Risdon Cove colony, a slump of rock, has become a counter-monument to invasion. It's an ecology, too. The dwellings and the memorial obelisk are decaying, surrounded by a commentary on their demise. 'For new stories to be told about Australia,' says Tony Birch, 'the colonial project of auto-monumentalisation has to be…reshaped.' Australians need forms of memory that 'get at the barely whispered and make it heard'.

Must it be painful? Writing about Holocaust memorialisation, James E. Young suggests that the 'texture' of memory can't be reduced to unchanging material form. Monuments represent 'collected memory' rather than 'collective' meaning; so how we treat them is how we animate those meanings, to see their multiplicity and tensions. Pain isn't a necessary part of the process, but it might be an inevitable one, at least some of the time. And the greatest pain will not be felt by those who have already been hurt and betrayed by denial. It will be felt by those of us conditioned to control the exhibit.

Unlike Country, a monument is ephemeral. It belongs to anybody. From the minute it stands up, a monument is already a ruin. Culture is acting upon it. It is something that anybody can make with anybody else. It can magnify what's on the ground, amplify it. Its life is being witnessed; and it is always asking what it will become next, for who comes next, 'through the very fact of having cared only for the present'.

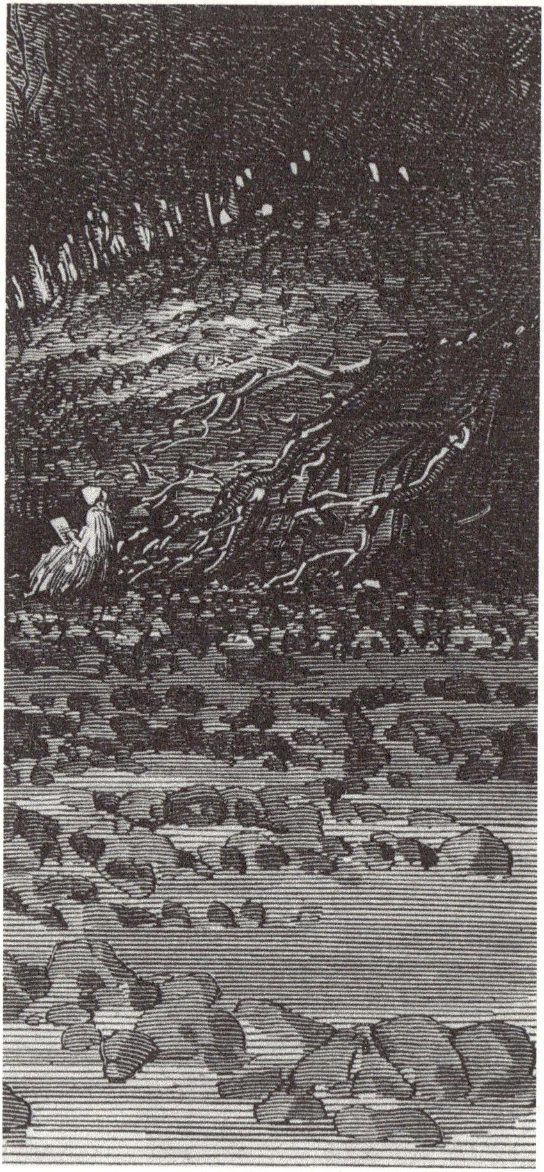

In his book *Minor Monuments*, the Irish author Ian Maleney says that 'writing, in the end, keeps us apart'. This is because, to 'put something into words at all is to manufacture a distance, a partiality, which is exotic, which turns memory into history'.

It's true, writing can thin the complexity of lives into a sentence. It binds us to the written word. Writing isn't memory. But it records things for revision; it makes me conscious of the passage between past, present, future. 'Only poetry preserves the force of unforgetting.'

First Nations writers in Australia already know this. 'We're writing the truth in our books as almost cement,' says the Yankunytjatjara poet Ali Cobby Eckermann.

I wonder what we settlers are doing with the truth in our books: pulling it further apart or putting it together for the first time? Am I cementing stories to fix them for good, or am I preparing for them to be dismantled, forgotten, when the time is right?

In 2019, the Tasmanian Museum and Art Gallery hosts a major exhibition, 'The National Picture'. The centrepiece of the show is Benjamin Duterrau's *The Conciliation*.

My mother's father had finally sold it to TMAG in 1945.

I sit in the gallery on one of those stiff black leather benches and watch.

Although the reputedly larger version of Duterrau's composition has never been seen, *The Conciliation* is still more impressive in scale than I'd remembered. It is so clearly made for a public institution, not a home. So, Duterrau got his wish to be a history painter – but not before his picture had lived its first century being smoked on and turned to the wall. I'm glad it got that chance at intimate life on a human scale.

Last century the painting was slashed seven times by a vandal. If the victim were human, I would call that frenzied. For a moment the picture became a monument – touchable, unfixed – before it was repaired and returned to a safe distance from the critics and artists continuing to interpret its ultimate significance.

For Richard Cleburne's daughters, on the other hand, the important thing was neither that it was lived with or appreciated, but that it was kept. Like any settler's heirloom, its continuity made them feel at home. Keeping may be a form of forgetting, too. My mother's father wanted to be recompensed for his keeping of the picture; for his own continuity to be given a price. To donate the picture to TMAG would have been to admit trespass.

/

Through the glass, it sees

solidifies
into furnishing like proof
of occupation, the right to be
portable, unmoving.

/

I stand and walk up to it, to see the brushstrokes. I get out my pen.
A museum attendant's body blocks the light

our shadows
interrupting one another

I am living on Dja Dja Wurrung land, closer
to some of the trees in my family.

I bought a shield that was made
where the spear was seen.

I chose the shield in defence, to walk into that picture of the past.

The shield was made in a prison, and its blackwood planed and glyphed with small spears of flame. To resist me, the oil from my hands shines the grain
and keeps my harm at length.

It's alive. It can't be framed.

I am flying over the peninsula of Dharawal lands, Gweagal lands. Salt-warped banksia and she-oaks on the low sandstone shelves at the mouth of the Port Hacking River. The concrete seafront boulevard, stucco surf clubs, bark-chipped playgrounds, and white-rendered flats. With a view towards Kurnell, where a headland of truck-stolen dunes still lies barely visible between stacks and tanks of the oil refinery. The fuselage of the *Mad Max: Beyond Thunderdome* aircraft lodged in the grains.

I hover. A bare, mown lawn that runs down to the South Cronulla surf break – its dark stain of reef, the night's tide hanging in the ocean pool, run-off draining through the sandstone.

The dream closes like sea-foam over sand.

I wake at my childhood home in Cronulla. I have come to help my mother pack up the house. While I'm in Sydney I will meet one of my sisters, who I have spoken with on the phone.

I walk through Gunnamatta Park and down to Darook Park. I'd believed that I could walk them in my sleep, they were so familiar. But they are changed.

The caves by the bay are scorched deep by fires – ancient ones staining the rock, and recent ones leaving ash. As I go around the peninsula to the mouth of the river, I see the old red brick house of a kindergarten friend. The Aboriginal flag drapes from its windowsill, mounted like a spotlight.

There is no national picture, and there never was. You'll never stand far enough back to see it all inside a frame. You can never see all the trees.

Because there's a story already happening
you are standing in it.

Someone knocks my shoulder. Runners and prams surge along the boulevard by the ocean. I've got time. I turn around and walk back the way I've come.

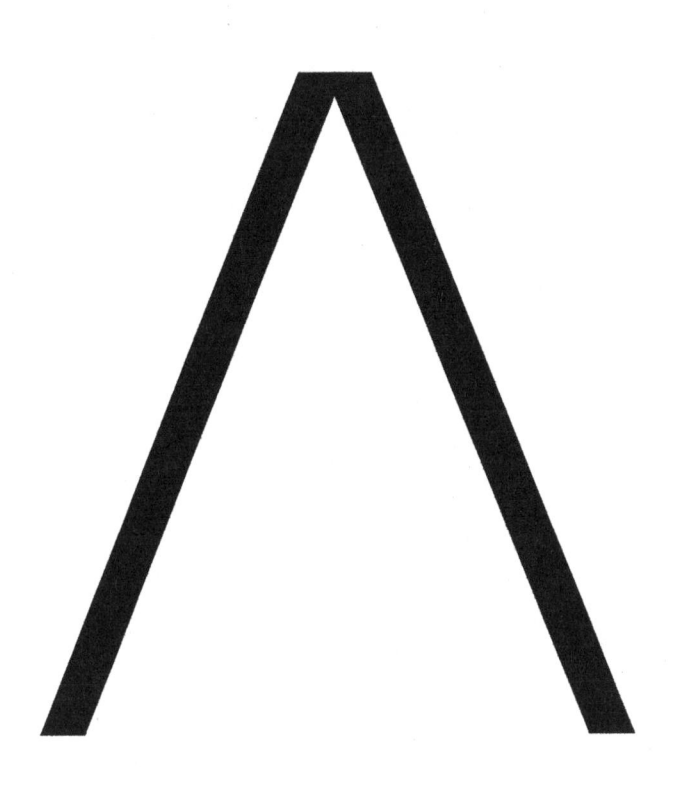

A note on the text

The research for this book began as a private path; enclosed.

While there were signs in stories and documents about some of my relations' lives, most of the first, second and even third generations in Australia were unlettered and untold. As I quickly found out, this ignorance is common amongst White settlers.

For a couple of years, I travelled around and riffled archives to learn those lives from scratch, or to test the well-trodden parts. I sought out people who I felt could help me gain an understanding of what and who were encountered by my family's first generations on already occupied continent. A way to bear witness, my searching grew into a fantasy of reconciliation. I would, I imagined, make deep connections with communities with whom my family has no living link. I would re-start the past.

Eventually, I realised that of course this fantasy could not be fulfilled. Writing a book could not stand in for such relationships. It could not be an express ticket to trust from communities that have often found their trust betrayed. And writing a book alone, no matter how many sources I consulted, would not constitute justice. Moreover, the fantasy was a distraction from what had become abundantly clear: I had to get my own story straight.

What I find in this book is a shadow text. A way towards something else. I still might have let this remain a personal store of reference and research, but it had already gotten away from me by connecting with other writings, histories and events that were taking shape out in the world. I have thought a lot about what non-Indigenous people might contribute to the growing wealth of First Nations truth-telling. This book stands adjacent. I think of it as storytelling and sometimes, when it's corroborated by sources that vary from colonial authorship, as history. While much of my work was meant to seek overlaps, the gaps in it show me what can be forgotten, what recovered, and what paths lie beyond the emblematic nature of a book.

My research and writing have been guided by the AIATSIS *Guidelines for the Ethical Publishing of Aboriginal and Torres Strait Islander Authors and Research from Those Communities* and Creative Australia's *Protocols for Using First Nations Cultural and Intellectual Property in the Arts*. This process, so much of which involves un-learning Western approaches to authorship, has been a rich education for me. Where I've fallen short, the responsibility lies with me. I welcome any correction or query concerning the research or content that isn't made clear.

A note on terms

There are a range of terms that I have used to identify distinct First Nations communities in Australia. When quoting the terms 'Aboriginal' or 'Indigenous', I do so to maintain the integrity of the source but otherwise I tend to avoid these generalisations. I have minimised quotation of derogatory terms from historical sources except where I believe it to be informative about the source or speaker. When speaking broadly at a regional, national or continental scale, I use the term 'First Nations' to indicate the multiplicity of Aboriginal cultures, language and traditions, not only distinct from one another but from settler colonial 'Australia'. Wherever possible I have preferred to use a language group or 'clan' name as correctly as I can or as it is used to self-identify by that community, e.g. Wergeia, Wotjobaluk. I don't pretend that I could get this perfect or that self-determined identities should conform to Anglophone rules. I would be pleased to be corrected or set straight.

Place names are used in line with the main historical perspective of each section. This means several places appear in the text by two names; a risk of confusion I decided to take so that the arbitrariness of colonial naming be obvious. Many places are presently in a transition, which is indicated with a comma denoting public acknowledgement of two naming systems. In some cases, like the Grampians/Gariwerd, dual naming has now been formally put in place. In lutruwita, Tasmania, the Tasmanian Aboriginal Centre freely shares palawa kani place names and they are used here with that permission. Palawa kani is the language of Tasmanian Aboriginal peoples: http://tacinc.com.au/pulingina-to-lutruwita-tasmania-place-names-map/

Source credits

Where quotations are not clearly attributed in the text, I've identified them below in order of appearance. I have also named just some of the directly influential work of others, who have taken this path before me. Where not otherwise noted, newspaper sources have been licensed under Copyright Agency's Open Licence. Except as permitted by the Copyright Act, work must not be re-used without the permission of the copyright owner or Copyright Agency.

'...the history of this country' (p. vii): Quotes Keith Windschuttle, *The Fabrication of Aboriginal History, Volume 1: Van Diemen's Land 1803–1847*, Macleay Press, 2002.

In the 1830s (p. 9) and **The Flinders Island settlement** (p. 11): I've drawn on Lyndall Ryan, *The Tasmanian Aborigines: A History Since 1803*, Allen & Unwin, 2012; and George Augustus Robinson, *Friendly Mission: the Tasmanian Journals and Papers of George Augustus Robinson, 1829–1834*, ed. N.J.B. Plomley, Queen Victoria Museum and Art Gallery and Quintus Publishing, 2008. Mudrooroo provides a powerful perspective on the mission in his novel, *Doctor Wooreddy's Prescription for Enduring the Ending of the World*, Hyland House, 1983. An excellent companion to the monument's construction is Clare Land, *Tunnerminnerwait and Maulboyheener: The Involvement of Aboriginal People from Tasmania in Key Events of Early Melbourne*, City of Melbourne, 2014.

John Curwen-Walker (p. 14): Stephen Scheding brought to light John Curwen-Walker's purchase of the painting, in *The National Picture*, Vintage, 2002. I've been influenced by Greg Lehman's significant criticism of the 'ekphrasis' involved in reading colonial history from artworks; and his sympathetic understanding of Duterrau's complex, ambiguous vision for 'the national picture'. I've drawn on Lehman's and

Tim Bonyhady's *The National Picture: The Art of Tasmania's Black War*, National Gallery of Australia, 2018.

Richard Cleburne will (p. 20): Quotes and draws from Nicholas Clements and Henry Reynolds, *Tongerlongeter*, NewSouth, 2021.

A monument may (p. 27): Quotes Stephen Muecke, 'A Touching and Contagious Captain Cook: Thinking History through Things', in *History, Power, Text: Cultural Studies and Indigenous Studies*, eds. Timothy Neale, Crystal McKinnon and Eve Vincent, CSR Books, 2014.

After a year or so (p. 36): Quotes Jaques Rancière, *Figures of History*, trans. Julie Rose, Polity, 2014.

My aunt gives me (p. 38): Quotes Rancière, *Figures of History*.

Wybalenna is miles behind (p. 44): Quotes Robinson, *Friendly Mission*; Ryan, *The Tasmanian Aborigines*; Inga Clendinnen, *Tiger's Eye*, Text Publishing, 2000.

In 1853 (p. 46): Quotes Nicholas Thomas, *Possessions: Indigenous Art/Colonial Culture*, Thames & Hudson, 1999; W.E.H. Stanner, *The Dreaming & Other Essays*, Black Inc, 2011; Paola Balla interviewed by Jana Perkovic, 'Blak Matriarchy', *Assemble Papers*, 26 April 2018. Draws on Statistics of the Colony of Victoria, 1853, Australian Bureau of Statistics Archive; and Luke Stegemann's distinction between forgetting and 'unknowing' in *Amnesia Road*, NewSouth, 2021.

Nan's family arrives (p. 50): Quotes in italics from James Dawson in Raymond Madden, 'James Dawson's Scrapbook: Advocacy and Antipathy in Colonial Western Victoria', *The La Trobe Journal*, 85 (May 2010); quotes without italics from John Cooper, *At the Hopkins: History of the Hexham District 1839–1989*, Royal Historical Society of Victoria, 1996. I've also drawn on Ben Wilkie, 'Landscapes of the Dead: History and Memory in a Distant Field of Murder', *Meanjin* Summer 2016.

What do they know? (p. 53): Quotes Bruce Pascoe, *Convincing Ground*, Aboriginal Studies Press, 2007.

My great-great-grandfather (p. 55): Quotes Aldo Massola, *Journey to Aboriginal Victoria*, Rigby Ltd, 1969; Caleb Collyer in Ian Clark, *Scars in the Landscape*, Aboriginal Studies Press, 1995; H.C. Builth, 'The Archaeology and Socioeconomy of the Gunditjmara: A Landscape Analysis from Southwest Victoria, Australia', PhD Thesis, Flinders University, 2002; Maggie MacKellar, *Strangers in a Foreign Land: The Journal of Neil Black and Other Voices from the Western District*, The Miegunyah Press, 2008; Tony Birch, '"Death is forgotten in victory": Colonial Landscapes and Narratives of Emptiness', in J. Lydon & T. Ireland, eds., *Object Lessons: Archaeology and Heritage in Australia*, Australian Scholarly Publishing, 2005; 'Cutting Up the Land: Its Progressive Effect', *The Age*, 31 March, 1910; Margaret Kiddle, *Men of Yesterday: A Social History of the Western District of Victoria 1834–1890*, MUP, 1963; Ross Gibson, *Seven Versions of an Australian Badland*, UQP, 2002; Lisa Slater, 'Waiting at the Border: White Filmmaking on the Ground of Aboriginal Sovereignty', in Beate Neumeier and Kay Schaffer, eds., *Decolonizing the Landscape: Indigenous Cultures in Australia*, Rodopi, 2014; Jan Critchett, *Untold Stories: Memories and Lives of Victorian Kooris*, MUP, 1998; Tony Birch, 'Come See the Giant Koala: Inscription and Landscape in Western Victoria', *Meanjin* 3 (1999); Land, *Tunnerminnerwait and Maulboyheener*.

The warfront (p. 64): Quotes George Augustus Robinson in Gary Presland, ed., 'Journals of G.A. Robinson, March 1841 – May 1841', Victoria Archaeological Survey, Aboriginal Affairs Victoria, 1977; University of Newcastle, Colonial Frontier Massacres in Australia: https://c21ch.newcastle.edu.au/colonialmassacres/map.php; Quotes Pascoe, *Convincing Ground*.

I buy thick-skinned lemons (p. 67): I draw from Varia Karipoff's interview, 'Hayley Millar-Baker Creates an Alternative Narrative', *Artguide* 20 June 2019. Quotes Michel Foucault, 'Nietzsche, Genealogy, History',

Language, Counter-Memory, Practice, ed. Donald F Bouchard, Cornell UP, 1977.

As a young woman (p. 69): Quotes Richard Zachariah, *The Vanishing Land: Disappearing Dynasties of Victoria's Western District*, Wakefield Press, 2017.

'Another Wimmera girl!' (p. 77): Quotes Paul Anders in Victor Rabl, *Early Murtoa History 1871–1983*, Murtoa and District Historical Society, New Style Publication, 1996; Keith C. Hofmaier, 'Aborigines in the Southern Mallee of Victoria', Paper, Royal History Society of Victoria, 1957, Manuscripts Collection; 'Vermin Destruction in Victoria', *South Australian Register*, 29 April 1893; Paul Carter, *Ground Truthing: Explorations in a Creative Region*, University of Western Australia Press, 2010; Peter Menkhorst and Edward Ryan, 'C.H. McLennan ('Mallee Bird') and His Aboriginal Informant Jowley: The Source of Early Records of the Night Parrot Pezoporus occidentalis in Victoria', *Memoirs of Museums Victoria* 73 (2015); Agnes Hilton, *The Mallee Pioneers of Hopetoun*, Hopetoun House, 1982; Alexander Sutherland, *Victoria and its Metropolis: Past and Present*, Today's Heritage, 1977; *Horsham Times*, 13 December 1892; H.P. Anders, 'Increasing the Wheat Yields', *Horsham Times*, 24 April 1900; Herman Anders, 'Mallee Settler's Suggestions', *Argus*, 15 October 1902. I use the idea of 'detritus' from Ross Gibson, 'Skerrick Scenes', in Gus Worby and Lester-Irabinna Rigney, eds., *Sharing Spaces: Indigenous and Non-Indigenous Responses to Story, Country and Rights*, API Network, 2006.

I've also drawn on Melissa Pouliot, *Yanga Track…Wanjab, Gadjin and Murnong*, Wimmera Catchment Management Authority, 2012; Anne Brown, *Wotjobaluk Dreaming: A Case Study of the Wotjobaluk People and Their Country*, Aboriginal Affairs Victoria and the Goolum Goolum Aboriginal Co-operative, 1999; Robert H. Stainthorpe and William Candy, *Early Reminiscences of the Wimmera and Mallee & Reminiscences of the*

Early Mallee and Wimmera, Lowden Publishing Co, 2009; Robert Kenny, *The Lamb Enters the Dreaming: Nathanael Pepper and the Ruptured World*, Scribe, 2007; Jon Rhodes, *Cage of Ghosts*, Darkwood, 2018.
Can I talk (p. 92): Quotes Tony Birch interviewed by Adele Sefton-Rowston, 'You'll Be Great, But Only If You Work Your Arse Off: An Interview with Tony Birch', *Overland*, 28 March, 2017. Skye Krischauff has done original work on intergenerational settler remembering and forgetting in *Memory, Place and Aboriginal-Settler History: Understanding Australians' Consciousness of the Colonial Past*, Anthem Press, 2017.
'The memory, monuments and memorials' (p. 95): Quotes Bill Gammage, 'Landscapes Transformed' in Marilyn Lake, ed., *Memory, Monuments and Museums: The Past in the Present*, MUP, 2006; Lidia Thorpe, 'Protecting the Djab Wurrung Trees', *The Saturday Paper*, August 17–23, 2019; Tiriki Onus, 'Reflections #32', Castlemaine Art Museum, 11 November 2020: https://us18.campaign-archive.com/?u=522abcffa55894025f026a224&id=87d124df0b; Lidia Thorpe in Le Grand, Chip, 'Tearing Down Statues Reveals Problem but No Solution', *The Age*, 13 June, 2020, licensed by Copyright Agency; Carter, *Ground Truthing*. The Dja Dja Wurrung shield incident is recounted by Gary Foley in *Goori Reader No. 1: History, Memory and the Role of Cultural Organisations in Entrenching Colonisation in Australia and Beyond*, Common Room, 2020.

This story was deeply enriched by the 'Counter-monuments' symposium at ACCA Melbourne, March 2020: https://acca.melbourne/counter-monuments-indigenous-settler-relations-in-australian-contemporary-art-and-memorial-practices/

Pieces of the bridge (p. 100): Alongside my own travel and research in the region, I was informed about trade, enlistment and political representation on the east coast of Aotearoa New Zealand by Michael King, *Penguin History of New Zealand*, Penguin, 2003.

Tom Nicholson (p. 106): Quotes Gregory Day, 'Mere Scenery and Poles of Light', *Island* 148 (2017); and Tom Nicholson in Brigid Magner's *Locating Australian Literary Memory*, Anthem Press, 2019. A vast critical study of Nicholson's work can be found in Amelia Barikin and Helen Hughes, eds. *Tom Nicholson: Lines Towards Another*, Sternberg Press, 2018. The contributions by Tony Birch and Jacqueline Doughty were especially useful to me.

Saltmills (p. 108): The Wathaurong context here is developed from Cahir, *My Country All Gone*.

While the hammer (p. 110): This is a found poem entirely collaged from newspaper articles containing the search terms 'Ballarat', 'diggings', 'white man' or 'natives' in the *Argus, Ballarat Star, Age, Bendigo Advertiser, Geelong Advertiser, South Australian Register, Adelaide Times, Horsham Times, Mount Alexander Mail, Examiner, Ballarat Courier, Illustrated Australian Magazine* issued between 1850 and 1906; and from the Victorian goldfields letters and journals of William Strutt, Eugene Von Guerard and contemporaneous documents cited in Cahir, *My Country All Gone: The White Men Have Stolen It – The Invasion of Waddawurrung Country 1800–1870*, Australian History Matters, 2019.

Thirteen years before (p. 120): Quotes George Augustus Robinson in Gary Presland, ed., 'Journals of G.A. Robinson, January 1840–March 1840', *Records of the Victorian Archaeological Survey* 5 (1977). I also learned much from Ian D. Clark, 'The Ethnocide of the Tjapwurong: The Nexus Between Conquest and Non-Being', BA Honours Thesis, Monash University, 1982.

The public holiday (p. 125): Quotes Polly Stanton, *Fossil*, Lost Rocks, 2021. Crossing back into Dja Dja Wurrung land from Wathaurong, I was thinking about Dhelkunya Dja, Joint Management Plan for the Dja Dja Wurrung Parks: http://www.dhelkunyadja.org.au/the-plan/joint-management-plan

I live in a valley (p. 127): Quotes from Aileen Moreton-Robinson, *The White Possessive*, University of Minnesota Press, 2015; Paola

Balla, 'Tyirrem; the end of the world as we knew it', *Sydney Review of Books*, 20 February 2020: https://sydneyreviewofbooks.com/essay/tyirrem-the-end-of-the-world-as-we-knew-it/. New perspectives on my neighbourhood in the Victorian goldfields came from Zvoncika Stanin, 'From Li Chun to Yong Kit: A Market Garden on the Loddon, 1852–1912', *Journal of Australian Colonial History* 6 (2004); and Bain Atwood's *The Djadja Wurrung, The Settlers and The Protectors*, Monash UP, 2017.

Cognitive dissonance (p. 137): Quotes Mark McKenna, *Looking for Blackfellas' Point*, UNSW Press, 2004; Gladys Milroy and Jill Milroy, 'Different Ways of Knowing: Trees Are Our Families Too', *Heartsick for Country: Stories of Love, Spirit and Creation*, eds. Sally Morgan, Tjalaminu Mia, Blaze Kwaymullina, Fremantle Press, 2008; Stanner, *The Dreaming & Other Essays*.

'...the inhabitants' (p. 139): Quotes 'Clarence Town', *The Australian*, 3 March 1847; Fintan O'Toole, *We Don't Know Ourselves*, Head of Zeus, 2021. I learned about the backgrounds of the girls from Western Sydney University, 'The Female Orphan School 1813–1850': https://www.westernsydney.edu.au/femaleorphanschool/home/the_female_orphan_school_1813_to_1850.

Back there (p. 143): Quotes O'Toole, *We Don't Know Ourselves*. I refer to Callum Clayton-Dixon's magazine, *Mugun & Gun: Resisting New England Frontier Wars – Edition One*, Anaiwan Language Revival Program.

I have no diary (p. 144): Quotes Milroy and Milroy, 'Different Ways of Knowing: Trees Are Our Families Too'.

We all know (p. 148): Quotes Kiddle, *Men of Yesterday*; Shipping – Passenger Lists, Various, 1839 Bounty Immigrants Index, Reel 1306 NSW State Records; *Glen Innes Examiner and General Advertiser*, 18 November 1884.

Terence and Jo (p. 154): The young men's journey was recounted by Terence Cassidy in 'A Record Trip with Cattle', *Glen Innes Examiner*, 4 December 1930.

In the centre of Armidale (p. 156): Quotes Judith Wright, 'South of My Days', *Collected Poems*, HarperCollins, 2016.

Mary makes it through (p. 160): This and the following stories about Mary Cassidy, Glen Innes, Beardy Plain and Tommy McPherson draw extensively on newspaper archives from Glen Innes between 1860 and 1900; Barry McDonald folklore collection 1970–89, Oral History, National Library of Australia; Callum Clayton-Dixon, *Surviving New England: A History of Aboriginal Resistance & Resilience through the First Forty Years of the Colonial Apocalypse*, Anaiwan Language Revival Program, 2019; Fabri Blacklock, 'Beyond Fabrication of Australia's History: A Documentation and Multi-Method Critical Analysis of Ngarabal and Biripi Elders', Paper, Perspectives and Experiences of Australian History, Brisbane, 03 – 06 December 2008, https://www.aare.edu.au/data/publications/2008/bla08741.pdf; Anna Cole, Victoria Haskins, Fiona Paisley, *Uncommon Ground: White Women in Aboriginal History*, Aboriginal Studies Press, 2005; Tim Rowse, 'Indigenous Heterogeneity', *Australian Historical Studies* 45 (2015). I also consulted a range of Anaiwan and Ngarabal sources held in the AIATSIS Collection, Canberra. Before I'd consciously thought of this book, Katrina Schlunke's *Bluff Rock: Autobiography of a Massacre*, Fremantle Arts Centre Press, 2005, was its headspring.

I'm a poor student of Irish but Manchán Magan offers a fantastic definition of the *púca* in his *Thirty-Two Words for Field*, Gill, 2020. Fitting as payback for the theft of a sign and for one who arrived on horse or cart, it is: 'an energetic manifestation that engenders fear in the dark or an apparition arising from the uncertainty sparked by the absence of light…

an indefinitely shaped evil spirit that goes about on all fours and carries victims off on its back'.

We imagine (p. 161): Quotes Clayton-Dixon, *Surviving New England*. I took courage from Stuart MacIntyre and Sean Scalmer, eds. *What If? Australian History as It Might Have Been*, MUP, 2006.

A sandy clearing (p. 177): While the Oban group's appearance at the show was documented, its content was not. For this I have drawn on acts and audience behaviour from public corroborees in other regions, in Maryrose Casey, 'Cross-Cultural Encounters: Aboriginal Performers and European Audiences in the Late 1800s and Early 1900s', *Double Dialogues* 14 (Summer 2011): http://www.doubledialogues.com/article/cross-cultural-encounters-aboriginal-performers-and-european-audiences-in-the-late-1800s-and-early-1900s/

I'm having lunch (p. 179): Quotes 'Deepwater', *Glen Innes Examiner*, 11 June 1901.

It takes a collective effort (p. 182): Quotes Bain Attwood, et al, *A Life Together, A Life Apart*, MUP, 1994. This section is based on Barry McDonald's important study of 'dying race' narratives in New England media, in 'You can Dig All You Like, You'll Never Find Aboriginal Culture There': Relational Aspects of the History of the Aboriginal Music of New England, New South Wales, 1830–1930, PhD Thesis, University of New England, 2000.

It's early evening (p. 184): Quotes Cassidy, 'A Record Trip with Cattle'; Chris Healy, *Forgetting Aborigines*, UNSW Press, 2008.

In *The Fabrication of Aboriginal History* (p. 189): Quotes Neika Lehman, 'Memorial', *The Black Brow* 40 (2018). My remark on creative memory draws on James E Young, *The Texture of Memory*, Yale UP, 1993.

In 1832 (p. 191): Quotes 'Original Correspondence', *The Tasmanian* 18 January 1833.

In 1840 (p. 192): Account given in Clements and Reynolds, *Tongerlongeter*.

In 1842 (p. 197): Account given in Clements and Reynolds, *Tongerlongeter*.
The survivors (p. 201): Quotes the *Hobart Town Advertiser*, 1 May 1855, in which Richard Cleburne's visit to Oyster Cove is noted. Curwen-Walker's sale was posted in the *Mercury*, Advertising, 14 October 1862.
I go further back (p. 205): Quotes TAC, '3rd May 1804 – waranta tangara takariliya mumirimina, lungkana risdon cove-ta': http://tacinc.com.au/3rd-may-1804/; Heather Sculthorpe interviewed on ABC Radio, 20 Feb 2015; Edward White in Ryan, *The Tasmanian Aborigines*.
I'm sitting in the dining room (p. 207): Quotes Kathy Marks, 'Channelling Mannalargenna', *Griffith Review* 39 (2013). I refer to the Crowther Reinterpretation Project: https://www.hobartcity.com.au/Community/Arts-and-culture/Public-art/City-of-Hobart-public-art-projects/Crowther-Reinterpretation-project. A thorough survey of Blak responses to monuments can be found in Bronwyn Carlson and Terri Farrelly, *Monumental Disruptions: Aboriginal People and Colonial Commemorations in So-Called Australia*, Aboriginal Studies Press, 2020.
The Conciliation (p. 211): Quotes a gallery catalogue note in Scheding's *The National Picture*.
The Cleburne women (p. 212): Credit for the comparison to Benjamin West's *Penn's Treaty* is due to Scheding, *The National Picture*.
Misses Emma and Louisa Cleburne (p. 213): Alison Alexander, *The Eastern Shore: A History of Clarence*, Rosny Park, 2003.
I'll start again (p. 214): Quotes Ghassan Hage, *White Nation: Fantasies of White Supremacy in a Multicultural Nation*, Pluto Press, 1999; Unknown author, biography of Richard Cleburne, private archive.
This archive loves (p. 216): Draws on Alison Ravenscroft, *The Postcolonial Eye: White Australian Desire and the Visual Field of Race*, Ashgate, 2012.
John was born (p. 217): Quotes and draws from United States passport application, US Foreign Service, Hobart, June 15 1903, National Archives, USA.

John is (p. 218): Important context from the American perspective comes from Scott Christianson's *Freeing Charles: The Struggle to Free a Slave on the Eve of the Civil War*, University of Illinois Press, 2010. Informed by Elizabeth Clark-Lewis, *Living In, Living Out: African American Domestics in Washington DC, 1910–1940*, Smithsonian Books, 2010; and Curwen-Walker family archive.

'One-Way Ticket' (p. 221): from *The Collected Poems of Langston Hughes* by Langston Hughes, edited by Arnold Rampersad with David Roessel, Associate Editor, copyright © 1994 by the Estate of Langston Hughes. Used by permission of Alfred A. Knopf, an imprint of the Knopf Doubleday Publishing Group, a division of Penguin Random House LLC. All rights reserved.

In 1894 (p. 223): Quotes James Baldwin, *Notes of a Native Son*, Penguin, 2018; Clark-Lewis, *Living In, Living Out*. Pulling the two continents together are Marilyn Lake and Henry Reynolds, *Drawing the Global Colour Line*, Cambridge UP, 2008; and Richard Waterhouse, 'The Minstrel Show and Australian Culture', *The Journal of Popular Culture*, Vol. 24(3).

While the Misses (p. 227): Quotes 'Entrants in Bass Solo Were All Baritones', *Examiner*, 3 April 1939; John H Hansbrough, 'Bismarck on Slavery', *Mercury*, 1 May 1896.

John even manages (p. 228): Quotes A.S.H. Weigall, 'The House Under the Hill', *My Little World*, Halstead, 1934; Cassandra Pybus, *Black Founders: The Unknown Story of Australia's First Black Settlers*, NewSouth Publishing, 2006. Draws from Richard Cleburne & Family Collection, Tasmanian Archives, Hobart.

In the 1880s (p. 229): Quotes Hansbrough, 'Bismarck on Slavery'. I considered ways of reading John's public letters in light of bell hooks' *Black Looks*, South End Press, 1992.

A letter to the editor (p. 231): Quotes Lake and Reynolds, *Drawing the Global Colour Line;* Sean Brawley and Chris Dixon, 'Jim Crow Downunder?

African American Encounters with White Australia, 1942–1945', *Pacific Historical Review*, Vol. 71, No. 4 (2002); 'Negro Disenfranchisement', *The Mercury*, 4 October 1895; 'Negro Outrages', *The North Western Advocate*, 9 December 1911.

Once he wrote (p. 232): John H. Hansbrough, 'Race Hatreds', *Mercury*, 28 February 1903. A global discourse is described in Clare Corbould, 'Black Internationalism's Shifting Alliances: African American Newspapers, the White Australia Policy, and Indigenous Australians, 1919–1948', *History Compass* 15 (2017); and Peter M. Sales, 'White Australia, Black Americans: A Melbourne Incident, 1928', *The Australian Quarterly* 46.4.

'My being is "known"' (p. 234): Quotes George Yancy, *Look, a White! Philosophical Essays on Whiteness*, Temple UP, 2012; Sales, 'White Australia, Black Americans'. Refers to J.H. Hansbrough, 'Russo-Jap Peace Terms', *Mercury*, 9 October 1905; and Fiona Paisley, *The Lone Protestor: AM Fernando in Australia and Europe*, Aboriginal Studies Press, 2012.

The memoirist (p. 236): Quotes Weigall, *My Little World*.

After the death (p. 238): Quotes letter by John H. Hansbrough to John Curwen-Walker, 14 November 1930, Curwen-Walker family archive; Pybus, *Black Founders;* letter by John H. Hansbrough to John Curwen-Walker, undated, Curwen-Walker family archive.

Whether or not Nan (p. 240): Quotes Bliss Broyard, *One Drop*, Hachette, 2007. I borrow the idea of the bystander from Anna Haebich, '"Between knowing and not knowing": Public knowledge of the Stolen Generations', *Aboriginal History*, Vol. 25, 2001. Bonyhady and Lehman quote my grandfather's correspondence from the TMAG archive, in *The National Picture*.

'Why are you here?' (p. 244): Quotes Reg Watson, 'Risdon Cove History Post-1803': http://regwatson.mydrive.me/; Email interview with Reg Watson, 25 January 2020; David Rieff, *In Praise of Forgetting*, Yale UP,

2016; Tony Birch in Barikin and Hughes, *Tom Nicholson*; Young, *The Texture of Memory*; Rancière, *Figures of History*.

In his book (p. 249): Quotes Ricoeur, *Memory, Forgetting, History*; Ali Cobby Eckermann interviewed by Astrid Edwards, The Garret Podcast, 19 August 2019: https://thegarretpodcast.com/ali-cobby-eckermann/

Image credits

Detail of *Hulk of the South Carolina in Risdon Cove*, date and photographer unknown, Tasmanian Archive and Heritage Office, PH30/1/26.
Detail of *Cleburne's Farm, Old Beach – built 1830s*, date and photographer unknown, Tasmanian Archive and Heritage Office, PH30/1/4188.
Detail of Tom Nicholson, *Towards a Monument to Batman's* Treaty, 2013–19, image by Christian Capurro courtesy of Tom Nicholson/Milani Gallery.
Detail of photograph of Hilda Helena Curwen-Walker née Squire, Cronulla, c1970s, photographer unknown, Cassidy family archive.
Display at Langi Morgala Museum, Ararat, Victoria © Bonny Cassidy.
William Strutt, *Black troopers escorting prisoner from Ballarat to Melbourne*, 1851, image courtesy of Parliament of Victoria.
Detail of portrait of 'Grandma Cassidy' Mary Cassidy née Sweeney, Glen Innes, New South Wales, date unknown, photographed by Edmund J. Sands, Roberts family archive.
Interior of verandah with Cleburne family, Risdon Cove, Tasmania, c. 1880s, photographer unknown, Curwen-Walker family archive.
Detail of *John Hansbrough – worked for Miss Cleburne, Mount Direction, Risdon*, 1910, photographer unknown, Tasmanian Archive and Heritage Office, NS933/1/40.
Detail of *Risdon Bay, Tasmania, with Mount Wellington in the Distance*, 1877, artist unknown, National Library of Australia, PIC Drawer 3181 #S3451.

Acknowledgements

I offer my gratitude to the traditional custodians of the unceded beaches and bays where I grew up: the Gweagal people of the Dharawal language group. My writing of this book was fed by the sovereign creeks, trees and skies of the Kulin nation, particularly the Boon Wurrung and Woi Wurrung language groups of Narrm, Melbourne, and the Dja Dja Wurrung of Central Victoria. I am grateful to their Elders and communities for the Welcome they extend to the rest of us who dwell there.

Thanks to my aunts, uncles, cousins and my brother who have helped make me. To my Nan, for nourishment and the potential of memory. To Mum, for making visual art my second home. To Dad, for the encouragement and education to write. And to TG, my brilliant friend.

/

My work is only a pebble among boulders.

Evelyn Araluen's criticism spurred me to consider the ability of a writer to bear witness. I didn't really know the right place to begin until the work of Professor Mark McMillan and Dr Peter West gave me tools to articulate co-existence. Encouraging words from Natalie Harkin and Ali Cobby Eckermann came, probably unbeknownst to them, at significant moments in the work's progress. Over a few years, Kat Clarke offered generous advice about researching the Wimmera Mallee, and an early remark of hers about self-care in this work has stayed with me all the way through.

As I went along, I was met by custodians and organisations who share their knowledges and Country with the public. Thanks to

Winda-Mara Corporation, Brambuk Cultural Centre and Koorie Heritage Trust for cultural tours on Country; and appreciation to Barry McDonald and the Oral History Unit at the National Library of Australia (NLA), and to Ian D. Clark and Australian Institute of Aboriginal and Torres Strait Islander Studies (AIATSIS) staff for permission to access their collections.

I have been privileged to meet individual researchers and keepers of information who volunteered their time and resources. These included: Veronica Williams for her Mary Sweeney and Cassidy genealogical research including permission to reproduce Mary's portrait; Eve Chappell at Beardies History House & Museum, Glen Innes; Judi Toms, Standing Stones Management Committee, Glen Innes; Caroline Chapman, Aboriginal History Research New England; Bill Oates, UNE Regional Archive; David Lander and Penelope Ann for the shared connection with the Cleburne household; Reg Watson for sharing his work and thoughts; and Sally Manuell and Peter Boyle for exchanging our mutual links to Emily Anders and Jabez Squire in Ararat and Aotearoa, with my deep respect for Sally's Māori ancestry.

To push the research along, I received Seed Funding from the Association for the Study of Australian Literature, and a Blindside Regional Residency at Mooramong National Trust Estate supported by Creative Victoria. My work in progress was supported by editors and producers who commissioned or published sections of this work as it progressed: André Dao (Reading Victoria); Ben Byrne (Avantwhatever Festival); Olivia Guntarik (TIMer app); City of Melbourne Knowledge Week; and Jacinta LePlastrier and John Kinsella (*Australian Poetry Journal*).

The many phases of writing have been so patiently and sympathetically shaped by readers who were willing to look at drafts. Every one of them advanced the realisation of my research and ideas with their insights. I am very grateful to: Brigid Magner, Jessie Webb, Shari Kocher, Catherine Harris, Lindsay Tuggle, Tim Grey, Prithvi Varatharajan, Tara Mordern-Paino, the RMIT non/fictionLab, Sarah Curwen-Walker, Joan Fleming, Oliver Shaw, Olivia Guntarik, Aleesha Paz and Ivor Indyk.

Finally, and most fundamentally, I acknowledge the words and ideas of the First Nations artists and thinkers that have provoked this writing and often appear in its pages. Uncle Jim Everett-puralia meenamatta gave permission to be named and generously read the lutruwita, Tasmania sections of the manuscript. Special thanks to Paola Balla, Tony Birch, Kat Clarke, Ali Cobby Eckermann, Neika Lehman, Hayley Millar Baker, Gladys Milroy and Jill Milroy/Fremantle Press, Aileen Moreton-Robinson/University of Minnesota Press, Bruce Pascoe/Aboriginal Studies Press and Alison Whittaker for permission to quote them or refer to their work here. I pay my utmost respects to this blazing constellation of intellects, to their Elders and Countries.

Author royalties and paid engagements earned from this book will be forwarded to Nalderun Education Aboriginal Corporation, Victorian Aboriginal Corporation for Languages and The Torch.

About the author

Bonny Cassidy is the author of three poetry collections – *Certain Fathoms*, *Final Theory* and *Chatelaine* (shortlisted for the Prime Minister's Literary Award for Poetry and the Judith Wright Calanthe Award) – and co-editor of the anthology *Contemporary Australian Feminist Poetry*. Her essays and criticism on Australian literature and culture have been widely published, and her awards include an Asialink fellowship and a Marten Bequest Travelling Scholarship. She teaches Creative Writing at RMIT University and lives in the bush on Dja Dja Wurrung Country, Central Victoria.